INDIE CRAFT

by Jo Waterhouse

LAURENCE KING PUBLISHING

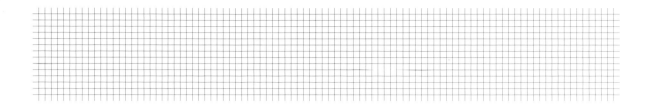

LAURENCE KING

Published in 2010 by Laurence King Publishing Ltd
361–373 City Road
London EC1V 1LR
United Kingdom
Tel: + 44 20 7841 6900
Fax: + 44 20 7841 6910
e-mail: enquiries@laurenceking.com
www.laurenceking.com

A catalogue record for this book is available from the British Library.
ISBN 978 1 85669 696 8

Design Charlotte Heal, www.charlotteheal.com
Senior Editor Clare Double
Editorial Director Jo Lightfoot

Printed in China

contents

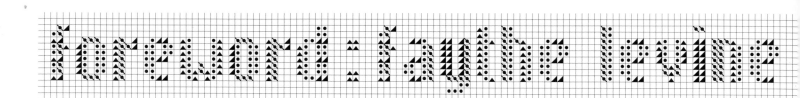
I was initially a holdout on the internet, so I find it somewhat ironic that my interest in handmade is what lured me into the World Wide Web and has now made me a devout fan. Barely ten years ago I used to feel that all correspondence should be done via handwritten letters and phone calls. I had spent years building up my correspondence with friends, sending ornately decorated letters and packages of every shape and form. A lot of these people I had met through the DIY punk scene that I grew up with in the early 1990s in Seattle. I would mail-order independently released zines (self-published magazines) and records, doing trades and forming relationships that have lasted until today.

It was 2002 when I started utilizing message boards, realizing that there was a vast network of people online – a part of the community that I related to. Websites such as getcrafty.com, cutxpaste.com and craftster.org were my first online stomping grounds within the DIY creative community. It was through these sites that I caught wind of what was being called an 'indie craft fair' in Chicago, called Renegade, that was looking for vendors. In September 2003 I participated in that show under my newly formed business, Flying Fish Design, which showcased my handmade goods. Little did I know that this single experience of meeting all these like-minded makers in Chicago face to face would change the course of my life.

What struck me at that first Renegade was the impact of the internet's ability to create community. It wasn't this evil thing that created space between people, as I had thought – it was a networking instrument that facilitated connections regardless of location. An organizer, like myself, could use this as a democratic dream weapon to make things happen.

I left that weekend excited and motivated. Within a year I had organized a craft fair in my hometown of Milwaukee called Art vs. Craft. Quickly following was the opening of Paper Boat Boutique & Gallery, a brick-and-mortar space that featured exclusively independent designers and artists.

I wasn't the only one who was inspired and motivated to make things happen; makers globally were utilizing the ever-growing resources online. They were also starting shows and opening shops as well as creating dialogue around the politics of handmade, sharing methods by posting images and tutorials of their creations. A large number of makers were also starting their own online shops as a way to bring in a second income, some going so far as to quit their day jobs to go full-time and head-first into this exploding DIY upsurge. The contagious feeling of the empowerment that DIY provides was spreading like wildfire.

My creative community was growing and seemed endless, and I knew that my community needed to be documented. There was too much amazing work, too much social change, too much not to capture it and share it with people who may not be familiar with the scene. Those of us involved who were continually struggling to explain that craft was something new needed a way to educate people. In 2006 I gathered my DIY ethos and enlisted my good friend, artist and filmmaker Micaela O'Herlihy. Without funding, we began a year-and-a-half-long journey to capture what was going on with the resurgence of handmade within the DIY art, craft and design community.

I tapped into my resources from my time spent online and started to spread the word that I was embarking on the journey of documenting what we were doing. I wanted to capture the energy, the politics, the makers and the work itself coming out of our creative generation. My peers were taking traditional methods and making them contemporary, and along the way educating the public that they too could pick up supplies and make something.

Craft-based work began to show up in high-end galleries, and former artists were shedding their titles and embracing the term 'maker'. Our community was changing the way that people ingest creativity, making it approachable and pushing design boundaries. We took craft to the street, reshaping a word that has, and will continue to have, many definitions.

Over the course of the three years I spent working on my documentary *Handmade Nation* I met most of the people I had only known online. My travels since completion of the film (and now book) have taken me around the world, ever further proving that craft can change lives. Art can heal. Making with your hands is empowering. As I continue to move forward as a maker myself, I am excited to see how our global community develops, and where we take this new trend of awareness and support. The thing that I have found about craft that I love the most, as my friend and colleague Andrew Wagner so eloquently put it, is that 'craft is what you make it'.

Faythe Levine
Director and co-author of *Handmade Nation*
www.handmadenationmovie.com

Introduction

The purpose of this book is to document Indie Craft: the fantastic art and craft work being produced by artists and makers using traditional craft techniques but with a completely modern, alternative and subversive style, context and subject matter.

The alternative craft scene is thriving and flourishing, especially since the advent of the internet, as Faythe Levine discusses in her foreword. Its roots are in the DIY punk scenes that came out of the United States in the early 1990s. Hence, alternative craft is often called DIY Craft, also to distinguish it from its traditional and twee-er forebear. Other names for DIY and Indie Craft are New Wave Craft, Subversive Craft and Craftivism (Craft + Activism – usually when the work contains more political or socially conscious subject matter). There are some subtle differences between all of these labels, but for the purposes of this book I'm taking an overview of the current, alternative, Indie Craft scene, meaning craft-based work that is alternative to the perceived, traditional craft subject matter. I'm specifically focusing on the superb work that is being produced by international artists and makers who operate independently, outside of 'mainstream' craft.

Contributing artist Jenny Hart's company Sublime Stitching sums up the Indie Craft aesthetic as 'This Ain't Your Gramma's Embroidery!' – meaning you won't find twee, traditional, mainstream designs – and the same goes for this book. There aren't any country cottages, cottage gardens or cutesy animals here, unless with a twist or a heavy dose of irony, such as artist Kate Westerholt's take on traditional cross stitch samplers.

As well as documenting the work being produced by artists and makers who work in traditional craft disciplines, but whose subject matter and finished pieces subvert the traditional craft genre, I have also included artists who have taken craft techniques to a new level and have blurred or completely broken through the line between art and craft. The idea is to present the work of artists/makers/crafters whose work straddles the alternative craft spectrum, from independent designer-makers who produce their own work to sell on Etsy.com through to gallery artists using traditional craft techniques in a new, unexpected and exciting way.

Artist Severija from Lithuania, for example, is an international gallery artist working with craft techniques. She works in cross stitch, but with drilled metal surfaces instead of the traditional fabric, deliberately choosing this discipline in order to:

raise doubt in the traditional hierarchy of art, between what is usually called 'high art' and less valuable art.

For any sticklers for details or definitions out there, her work wouldn't really be considered 'DIY Craft' given her contemporary art background and context, and she doesn't consider herself a craftsperson, but I really wanted to include her work here as it is a surprising, intriguing and alternative take on craft techniques, and therefore to my mind can also be considered Indie Craft in the context of this book.

The 'art vs. craft' debate is old and multi-faceted. I prefer to leave that discussion up to the individual. Art by its nature is wholly subjective, and I believe that all of the pieces in the book can be viewed as either art or craft, or both. The decision should in part be determined by the intention of the creator, and is partly up to the viewer and how they naturally respond to and interpret it.

For this book I have predominantly focused on artists who work with textiles or fibre, using knitting, crocheting, felting, fabric/plush toy-making, hand embroidery, machine embroidery and cross stitch. That's not to say that the terms Indie/New Wave/DIY craft don't also apply to every other craft discipline out there, but due to the size

and space in the book I decided to narrow the focus.

Indie/DIY craft can be viewed as a response to the homogenous mass production and mass consumption that is synonymous with the modern world. The scene's continued rise in popularity can also be attributed to the current economic and environmental crises we face. As Magda Sayeg of Knitta Please puts it:

I'm part of the DIY craft movement that emphasizes handmade artistry as a reaction to the mass-produced culture we're immersed in.

If you make handmade items, whether for practical reasons (clothing or home wares), for decorative reasons, or as gifts, you are turning your back on the mass-produced items found on most high streets or in shopping malls. You are creating something unique, personal and special. A lot of indie crafters/artists use recycled or vintage materials, and making something yourself by hand from recycled materials obviously has less impact on the environment.

Textile-based crafting has traditionally been seen as a domestic, female-dominated (if not exclusively female) hobby or pastime and usually not as an art form in its own right. Several Indie Craft artists are striving to change that perception. As embroidery artist Jenny Hart explains:

Embroidery serves no function, and is almost always secondary to a functional object (a pillowcase; a tea cosy). As an artist, one of my considerations is to make this type of needlework embellishment the substance of the subject and the object itself.

Berlin-based crochet artist Patricia Waller comments:

Wool is ranked low in art and art history. It is not the material from which major works of art were made, and it is considered feminine,

Artists choosing to work with traditional craft materials and techniques and the rise of the Indie Craft scene are helping to change this perception by contrasting craft methods with non-traditional subject matter and in a non-traditional context, for example, a gallery space or a street. Subject matter chosen by Indie Craft artists tends to be much less feminized and feminine than traditional decorative craft subject matter, and as a result there are more and more men coming out of the craft closet. This book features four male artists: Phil Davison, founder of Urban Cross Stitch; Matte Stephens, a needle felter; Howie Woo, a 3D crocheter, and William Schaff, an embroiderer. Men who participate in embroidery often have their work entitled 'manbroidery' or 'emBOYdery', and there are often distinguishable elements of masculinity in the subject matter and tone of these artists' work. For instance, Phil Davison recreates Banksy graffiti as cross stitch patterns, while Howie Woo crochets rayguns and grenades. It's this juxtaposition of traditional craft technique and, in this case, masculine and urban subject matter, that makes the work stand out as Indie Craft.

Any feminists who have bemoaned the current rise of craft shouldn't worry, as both men and women are partaking in the new wave. Indie Craft isn't about keeping women busy, as it may have been in previous centuries, and it isn't purely decorative art. Today's craft is also about empowerment: feeling a sense of achievement when making something with your own hands. It's about taking a stand or making a statement against this modern, digital, disposable age of mass production and consumption that is leading the world into environmental and economic ruin. It's about creating something you might not have 'needed' to make yourself – you could have gone to any shop and bought, for instance, an (unfeasibly, unsustainably) cheap, mass-machine-made scarf or jumper – but that gave you the sense of achievement and empowerment that comes from learning and perfecting a skill, making a unique item by yourself, for yourself or for a gift, and in many cases making a small, independent business out of your creations. Part of the Indie Craft ethic involves supporting independent artist-designer-makers and supporting the idea of a society where artists can make a living from their creations and where independent creative businesses can flourish.

Community is a big part of the Indie Craft scene, expressed in online communities, local/regional events, and groups and collectives. Therefore I wanted to include in the book a few collectives and those involved with 'communi-crafting' events. We feature the Craft Guerrilla collective; Phil Davison, who holds Urban Cross Stitch event nights; and graffiti knitters Knitta Please and Knit the City. With Indie/New Wave/DIY craft, it couldn't be easier to find like-minded craft-artists and join local groups or even start one yourself. There are many umbrella groups and collectives out there that allow you to start a group under their name, including Craft Guerrilla, Craft Mafia, The Church of Craft, and Stitch 'n' Bitch. DIY craft is all about making things happen for you and in your area; if there isn't anything going on yet near you, start your own faction, or put on your own Indie Craft fair and events: you'll be surprised how many New Wave Crafters will come out of the woodwork!

The format of this book has deliberately been kept small and affordable. It serves as an introduction to each of these artists' work and the subject matter as a whole, and is not meant to be a detailed tome or encyclopedia – it merely scratches the surface of the amazing work being produced by talented Indie Crafters, alternative craft-artists and artists working with craft techniques. There are many 'how-to' craft books out there, and the Indie Craft scene and people behind the work have been documented wonderfully in the film and book *Handmade Nation*, so the focus of this book is purely in the craft-art work itself.

For those previously unfamiliar with the notion of Indie Craft, you can use this book as an introduction to the Indie

Craft scene and the work therein, and as a launch pad for further reading and investigation. It is also intended as an inspiration and incentive to take up Indie Crafting, providing examples of how much can be achieved with traditional craft techniques, and how these conventional techniques can be applied in unconventional ways with incredible results. For those already immersed in the scene, this book is a documentative snapshot of the wonderful work coming out of the alterative craft-art world and describes how the handmade and alternative craft movements are important and relevant today in a wider cultural, social and environmental context.

Jo Waterhouse

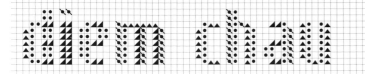

diem chau

Diem Chau is based in Seattle, USA, but is originally from Ho Chi Minh City in Vietnam, having come to the United States with her family as refugees in 1986.

Diem grew up surrounded by sewing and embroidery, as her mother was a seamstress. Although she studied art, graduating from Cornish College of Arts with a BFA in 2002, the techniques she uses today are self-taught and learned through books, friends and family. She believes that 'experimenting and giving yourself the permission to fail is a must in learning'.

Diem embroiders her designs onto silk, then attaches the silk to porcelain, which she collects from thrift stores. The resulting work is unique and has a delicate and fragile feel to it. From a distance the porcelain itself appears embroidered. She describes the process and her inspirations in her own words:

I usually make sketches of family photos. Then I decide on my composition by overlapping the sketch and the plates or cups. A piece of silk is pinned to the sketch and I embroider on the silk. After the embroidery is done I mount the silk to the plate using archival glue. The subjects of my work come from old family photos, but I deliberately pick out people I don't know. I like the sense of closeness, but at the same time they are strangers as well.

Diem describes her work as combining 'common mediums and common means to create delicate vignettes of fleeting memory, gesture and form'.

Diem's work has been featured in *Harper's*, *Fiberarts*, *Readymade* and *Seattle* magazines, and she has exhibited widely with shows in New York, Miami, Seattle and Los Angeles.

As well as her embroidery work, Diem also makes small, delicate carvings into crayons and loves to knit and crochet for fun.

I do everything from welding to sewing. I like to learn new skills and work with different materials. I decided to become an artist after my father's death when I was in high school. I wanted to spend my life doing something I love. But I started carving crayons and embroidering on porcelain about five or six years ago. I wanted to work with everyday materials and work outside of the 'art' realm.

www.diemchau.com

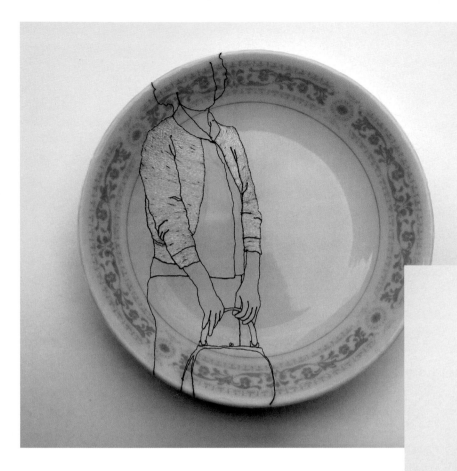

 **PREVIOUS PAGE, CLOCKWISE FROM LEFT:**
All images are ceramic plate, silk, thread.

LEGACY
FLOAT
Positioning the design on the ceramic plate.
Positioning the silk over the design.
Embroidering the silk.

LEFT TO RIGHT:
All images are ceramic plate, silk, thread.

DEPARTURES
SOJOURN
GRASP

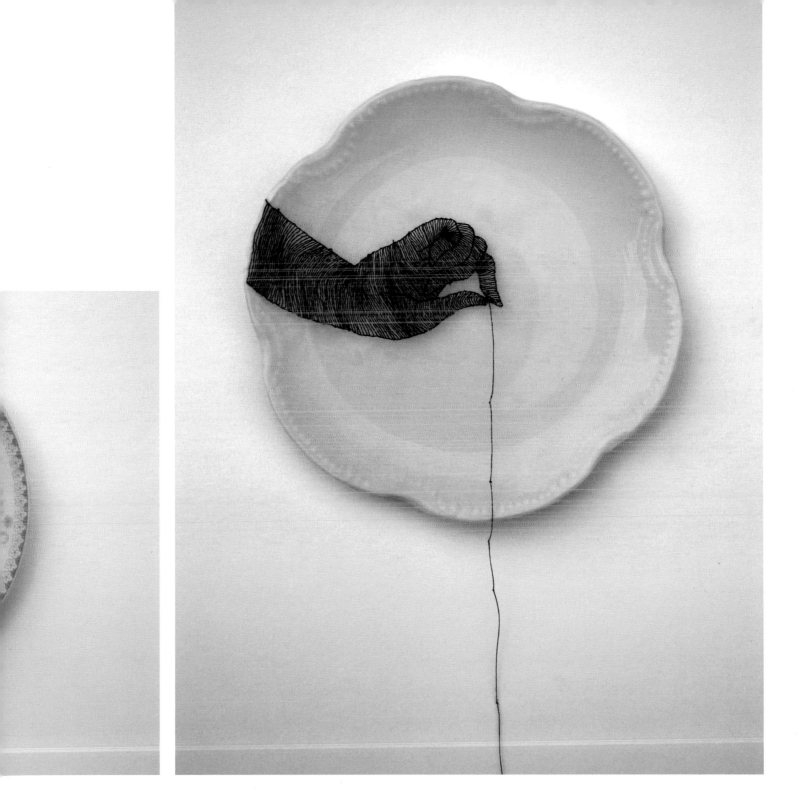

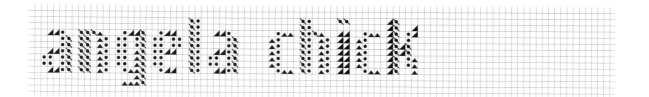

angela chick

Angela Chick is based in Brighton, England (via Surrey, England and Nova Scotia, Canada). She currently utilizes screenprinting, free machine embroidery, hand embroidery and illustration in her work, but is always looking to learn and implement new skills and techniques.

Angela has been making things for as long as she can remember. She has a creative mother and a grandmother who taught textiles and was always teaching her different embroidery and knitting techniques.

Angela started off studying Fine Art/Design in Ontario, Canada, but transferred to studying Craft and Design with a focus on Textiles after realizing that her passion lay with textiles and craft techniques. Before completing that course, she returned to the UK to live and studied for a BA in Textiles at the University for the Creative Arts in Farnham, where she gained a First.

Angela describes her work as illustrative, playful and interactive. Her projects include practical items such as cushions, purses, pouches and wallpaper. The interactive nature of her work comes from her collaborations with strangers on her wallpaper and cushion projects:

In my wallpaper project I was collecting secrets from strangers, and that was awe-inspiring. Knowing that people who had no idea who I was would tell me some of their deepest, darkest secrets was absolutely astounding. It became addictive. In my next project I created cushions that were designed from drawings of people's collections. I had requested people to send me photographs of their collections. It was such an amazing thing to be able to see into a stranger's room, and their prized possessions. Collecting and collections play a big part in my work.

Angela's working process can be lengthy and time-consuming. She is also committed to working with recycled materials wherever possible:

Anything recycled is my preferred material. This may mean I travel to various charity shops until I find that perfect piece, or simply root through a friend's closet. The only sad thing about using recycled materials is that when it's gone, it's gone.

I spend a lot of time collecting and contextualizing before pen goes to paper. I like to research a lot. This means spending hours leafing through magazines, and piles and piles of books. Once I feel like I've researched something so that I understand it as best as possible, that is when I begin to draw. I use a lot of fine line in my work and it is therefore important to me that I get my lines exactly as I want them to be. Once I have chosen a design, I screenprint it onto my chosen fabric. In the past I have hand-dyed fabrics before printing, and sometimes printed onto raw, undyed fabrics. Once I have decided on the composition, I print my final piece. After the final piece is printed, I use free machine embroidery to embellish it and finally hand embroidery to add any finishing touches. It is always important that my work is tactile and this calls for details that people can explore, such as subtle changes in texture, and the perfect fabric.

Angela is one of the founding members of Brighton Craft Guerrilla – a sister 'army' to the Craft Guerrilla umbrella collective.

www.angelachick.com
www.brightoncraftguerrilla.blogspot.com

◢ **ABOVE:**
MY PLACE OR YOURS? CUSHIONS
Recycled fabric, screenprint, machine embroidery, hand embroidery.

LEFT:
MY PLACE OR YOURS? CUSHIONS AND WALLPAPER
Paper, screenprinted line drawings.

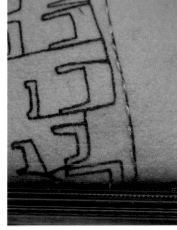

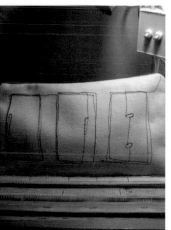

▲ **CLOCKWISE FROM FAR LEFT:**
Angela holding a My Place or Yours cushion.

MY PLACE OR YOURS? WALLPAPER
Paper, screenprinted line drawings.

MY PLACE OR YOURS? POUCHES
Recycled tactile fabrics, screenprint, machine embroidery, hand embroidery.

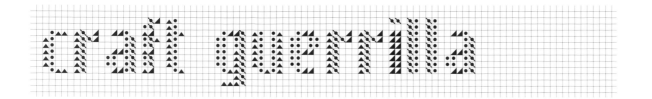

craft guerrilla

Craft Guerrilla was founded in January 2008 by core members Debbie Daniel (who is originally from Portugal and also works under the name Munano), Lisa Margreet Payne and Louise Batten. They explain:

We're basically a collective set up by designer-makers for designer-makers. We host craft markets, Crafternoons and DIY craft nights. All our events are set up to benefit the designer-makers who are involved, to share craft knowledge and to do it in a fun way with the general public. Our craft nights normally have guest DJs, vintage board games and guest tutors. We like mixing it up and making it an easy-going event that is relaxing, social and fun!

Craft Guerrilla are an umbrella group that encourage other 'sister armies' to share their manifesto and start up in other areas of the country. So far Craft Guerrilla has three sister armies, in East London (home of its founders), Brighton and Edinburgh.

The East London Craft Guerrilla's members work in a variety of media. Debbie practises a wide variety of craft disciplines, from embroidery and knitting to printing. Under her Munano moniker she produces plush characters or 'kawaii' soft sculptures. She comments:

Kawaii is a Japanese term and I think it is best described as cute with a dark side! I love felt, tweed and recycled vintage fabrics. Curtains are great, as they're hard-wearing and you get lots for your money.

Another East London Craft Guerrilla member is Ariane Dreysse, a.k.a Peppermint Twist. She says:

I love sewing and make purses and bags in soft leathers and fabrics under the moniker Peppermint Twist. I am very fond of all visual art forms, especially fashion, films and painting. My designs are quirky and one-of-a-kind; recently my work has moved towards playful and toy-like colours.

East London Craft Guerrilla have participated in the E17 Art Trail for two years running ('Hearts for the Heartless 2008' and the 'Craftea Party 2009'); the 'Cut-Click' anniversary exhibition at the Abbey Walk Gallery in Grimsby; and 'Make and Mend' at the Bury St Edmunds Gallery in the capacity of craft tutors.

www.craftguerrilla.com
www.eastlondoncraftguerrilla.blogspot.com
www.munano.co.uk
www.pepperminttwist.co.uk

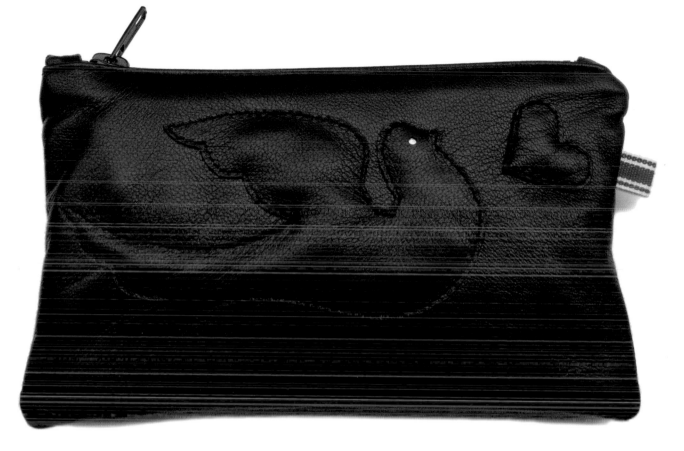

LEFT:
CHANGE PURSE, by Peppermint Twist
(Ariane Dreysse)
Aqua and dark silver.

ABOVE:
BLACK ZIP POUCH, by Peppermint Twist
(Ariane Dreysse)
Black dove appliqué, reclaimed leather.

RIGHT:
ZIP POUCH, by Peppermint Twist
(Ariane Dreysse)
Silver horse appliqué, reclaimed leather.

CLOCKWISE FROM RIGHT:

ANTON 'TONY' JET SQUIRREL,
by Munano (Debbie Daniels)
Felt, stuffing, appliqué, embroidery,
hand and machine sewing.

GNARLY BEAR VINTAGE FABRIC,
by Munano (Debbie Daniels)
Stuffing, vintage buttons, felt appliqué,
hand and machine sewing.

Craft Guerrilla members at the 'Make
and Mend' exhibition at the Bury St
Edmunds Gallery exhibition.

HEART PIN CUSHION, by Debbie
Daniels for E17 Art Trail.
Printed felt.

MORI MORI, by Munano
(Debbie Daniels)
Tweed, felt, beads, stuffing, appliqué,
hand and machine sewing.

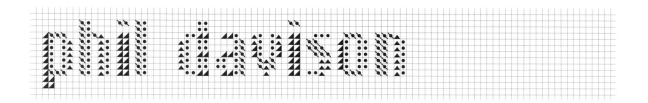

phil davison

Phil Davison is originally from Belfast, Northern Ireland, via Arkansas, USA, but he is now based in East London. He founded Urban Cross Stitch in August 2008 as a way 'to introduce the therapeutic process of cross stitch to an otherwise disinterested generation while simultaneously introducing street art to an otherwise disapproving generation'. He uses modern-day images such as pictures of street art by Banksy, computer games or references to contemporary society in his cross stitch designs for the discipline to appeal to a new and younger audience. He says:

I was taught how to cross stitch in Arkansas around Christmas 2007 by an elderly family friend, to help me relax from the stresses of the fashion industry. I immediately fell in love with the therapeutic process of cross stitching, but not so much with the designs available to stitch. Unable to find cool cross stitch designs with an updated aesthetic (anything other than puppies, unicorns and cottages), I was inspired on returning to London in 2008 to combine my new-found love of cross stitch with my existing love of street art. I launched Urban Cross Stitch in August 2008, taking cross stitch in a new direction with hip, updated patterns.

Preparatory work for Phil's pieces varies for each one. The pieces can be inspired from photos of street art he has taken on his travels, something he has seen on TV, or references to pop culture:

Either way I will start with an image, either a photo or drawing I have done, then I will work out a colour scheme for the piece. I pixelate the image using Photoshop and then, using graph paper and coloured pencils, I work out the image until I am happy with the overall look. Then I stitch the initial design to work out thread counts and see if it actually looked like how I wanted it to. Most of the time it does. I use the basic 'X' cross stitch. This involves stitching a row of half-stitches left to right such as /////////, then returning right to left stitching the second half-stitch such as \\\\\\\\\\, therefore making a row of full stitches such as XXXXXXXXXXXX. There is

nothing more complicated than that in any of my designs. I like low-fi! Keep things simple is my philosophy. Urban Cross Stitch: five minutes to learn, a lifetime to enjoy!

Urban Cross Stitch host regular 'Cupcakes! Cocktails! & Cross Stitch!' events in East London. They always welcome new members who want to learn cross stitch or who want advice or tips from other cross stitch enthusiasts.

www.urban-cross-stitch.com

■ **CLOCKWISE FROM LEFT:**
MAKE MY DAY
Cross stitch, cotton floss, Aida fabric.

BANKSY'S FLOWER BOMBER
Cross stitch, cotton floss, Aida fabric.

BANKSY'S THUG FOR LIFE
Cross stitch, cotton floss, Aida fabric.

BANKSY'S BRICK WALL MAID
Cross stitch, cotton floss, Aida fabric.

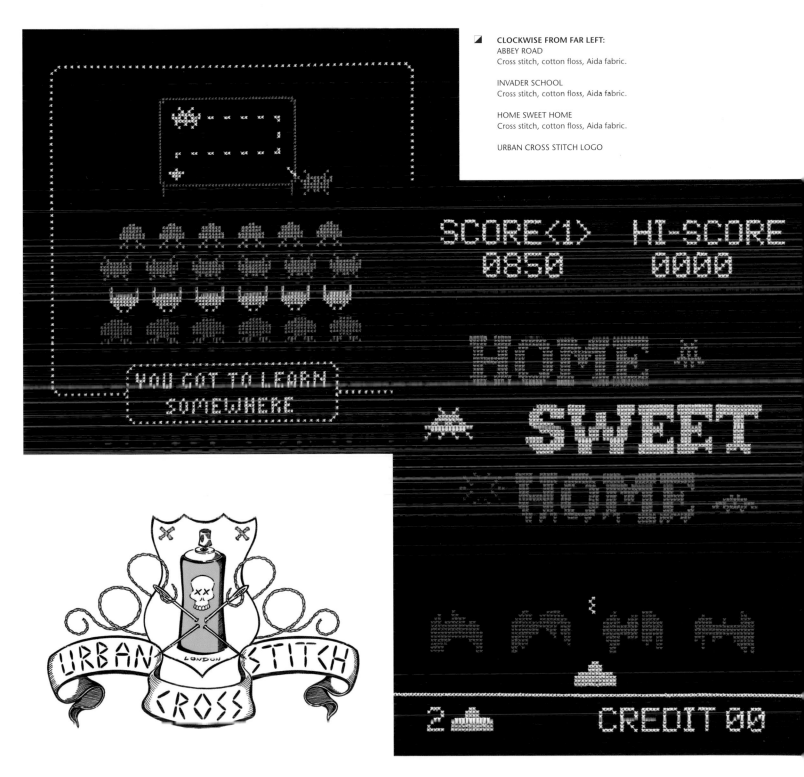

CLOCKWISE FROM FAR LEFT:
ABBEY ROAD
Cross stitch, cotton floss, Aida fabric.

INVADER SCHOOL
Cross stitch, cotton floss, Aida fabric.

HOME SWEET HOME
Cross stitch, cotton floss, Aida fabric.

URBAN CROSS STITCH LOGO

YOU GOT TO LEARN SOMEWHERE

SCORE<1>   HI-SCORE
0850   0000

HOME SWEET HOME

URBAN CROSS STITCH
LONDON

2   CREDIT 00

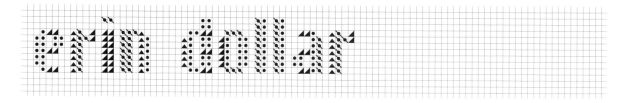

erin dollar

Erin Dollar is from Portland, Oregon, USA. She considers herself an artist and a crafter, although primarily she is a printmaker. She began making her beards three years ago. She explains:

My beard project is extremely playful in nature, but makes a subtle statement about gender roles and what women are expected to make as craftspeople. I am always inspired by people who do things differently, who go against the grain. In terms of beard-related influences, I think Frida Kahlo and Edward Gorey are my two biggest influences, in terms of the frame of mind I am in while I create things. Kahlo is such an inspiration to me; she seemed so strong in her convictions about who she was, and wasn't afraid to show it. Gorey's twisted stories and detailed drawings have always inspired me, and showed me at an early age that it was okay to imbue your art with humour. Plus, both Kahlo and Gorey had excellent facial hair.

The best part of making fake beards is the awkward glances I receive when I wear them. I want the beards to start conversations, to evoke a double take. While they are incredibly playful in nature, I also create the beards with the intent to explore social constructions of gender and my own experience of femininity. By creating a wearable beard, I am breaking into the traditionally male pastime of beard-growing, something that women are genetically and socially excluded from. In using yarn, felt and wool to create the beards, I combine the stereotypically feminine act of crafting and sewing with the deviation of entering into a male domain by creating and wearing a beard.

Erin studied printmaking at University of California Santa Cruz, graduating in 2008. She found mentors there who encouraged the playful side of her work, and she didn't feel any pressure to 'get serious' with her art and give up on the humorous elements of her work.

Each one of her beards is a little different from the last as she finds new ways to improve on each one. At this point her beards are made from the same basic template, which took time to get right:

It took a while to develop a template and a technique that seems to fit most people in a flattering way, but after I figured that out, it has been really easy to try new things and experiment with new materials or styles. In the beginning, I would sew each piece of yarn onto the lining by hand, which took hours to finish. It took a few tries, but I finally figured out a way to do most of the sewing on a machine, making the beards much more sturdy. Most of the process is streamlined now, which is great, as it allows me the time to search for new materials and work on new projects. I love working with inexpensive materials like felt and yarn, and I think that the accessibility of the materials is part of what makes this project so much fun. I don't have to worry about 'messing up', or ruining expensive materials if I don't like the outcome.

www.imadeyouabeard.com
www.imadeyouabeard.etsy.com

CLOCKWISE FROM BELOW:
BLACK YARN BEARD
Yarn, felt and ribbon, machine and hand sewing.

GREY ZEUS BEARD
Grey felt and ribbon, machine and hand sewing.

SEA FOAM GREEN BEARD
Yarn, felt and ribbon, machine and hand sewing.

CHAMPION BEARD,
AFTER JACK PASSION
Yarn, felt and ribbon, machine and hand sewing.

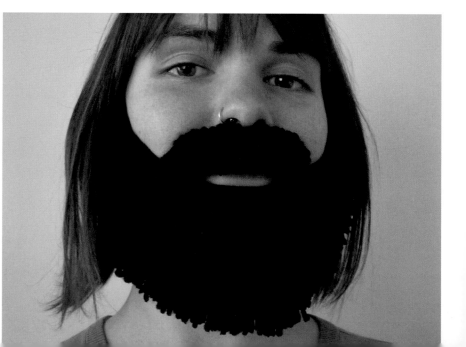

LEFT TO RIGHT:
HONEY BEARD
Yarn, felt and ribbon, machine and hand sewing.

BROWN YARN BEARD
Yarn, felt and ribbon, machine and hand sewing.

SOFT GREY BEARD
Unspun wool roving, felt and ribbon, hand-sewn.

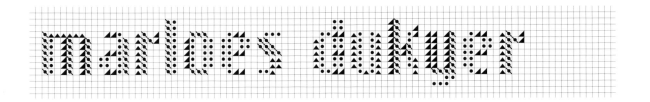

marloes dukyer

Marloes is from Heemskerk, a small town in the northwest of the Netherlands. She is now based in Utrecht, where she studied illustration at the Utrecht School of the Arts.

Marloes describes her work as a fusion between fashion, art and illustration. She uses a regular sewing machine like a pencil, to freehand machine sew and embroider her pieces. She also often sews onto transparent fabric and weathered watercolour paper ('I just put the paper between piles of wet leaves in my garden for a while') in order to create unusual backgrounds for her work. She adds:

I started working with the sewing machine during my studies at art school. Before then, I used many different styles and techniques, figuring out which style suited me most. During my studies I was stimulated to experiment with all kinds of unconventional materials, since illustrating is much more than a pencil drawing or a painting. I tried to work with the sewing machine as a device to make an image. The results were beautiful; very surprising and stimulating. I was thrilled, as I had found my way to make innovative and refreshing images. I love the tactility, the warm image and the texture of the material, especially in the present-day cold, digital era.

Marloes is inspired by many things, particularly nature; she has a fascination for mould, moss and decay, which is apparent through her use of weathered materials and her experimentation with sewing onto tree bark. Her working process is also organic and experimental:

I hardly ever make sketches before I start making an illustration. I never really know what it will look like in the end because I improvise a lot and let coincidence take its course. Sometimes I take out materials without even looking and come to interesting combinations of colours and structures. The sewing machine is quite crude if it is used in the way I do. I use this to my advantage. It gives my work spontaneity. Sometimes the machine messes up things to my advantage. I call these mistakes beauties of imperfection; they make the image lively. I also mostly leave 'waste' threads for the same purpose.

Marloes set up her own design agency, Naked Designs, in 2004 and has worked for high-profile clients such as Volvo, Vodafone and Tommy Hilfiger, among many others. She has also provided illustrations for numerous magazines and books as well as exhibiting her work widely. She is currently working on a collection of sewn accessories to be sold at shops, galleries, her Etsy store and through her website.

www.nakeddesign.nl

LEFT:
WINDOW AREA
Machine sewing on fabric.

RIGHT:
SWEET FINGER
Machine sewing on fabric, lace,
mixed media.

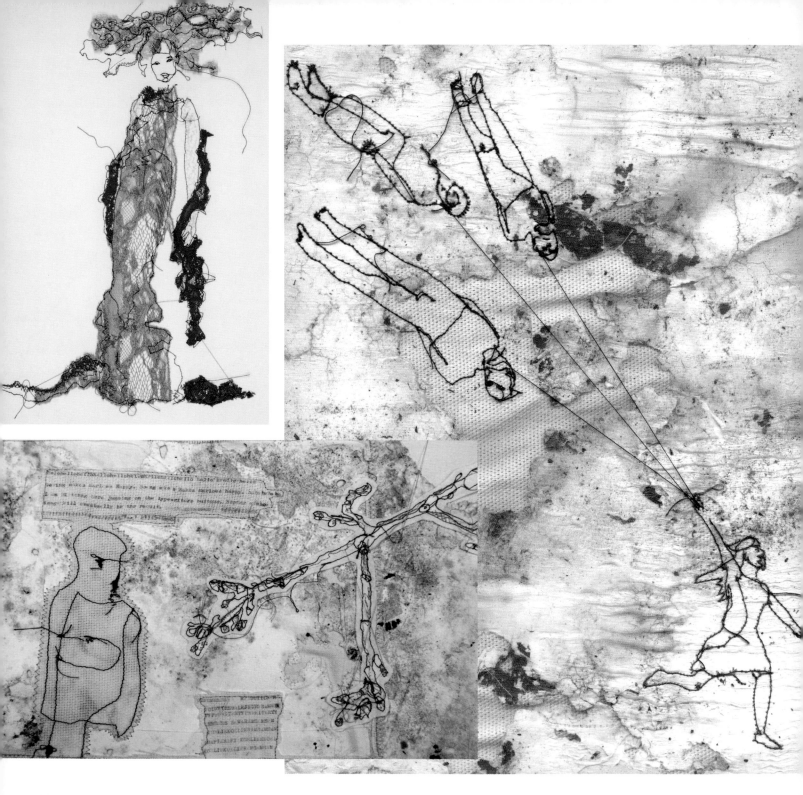

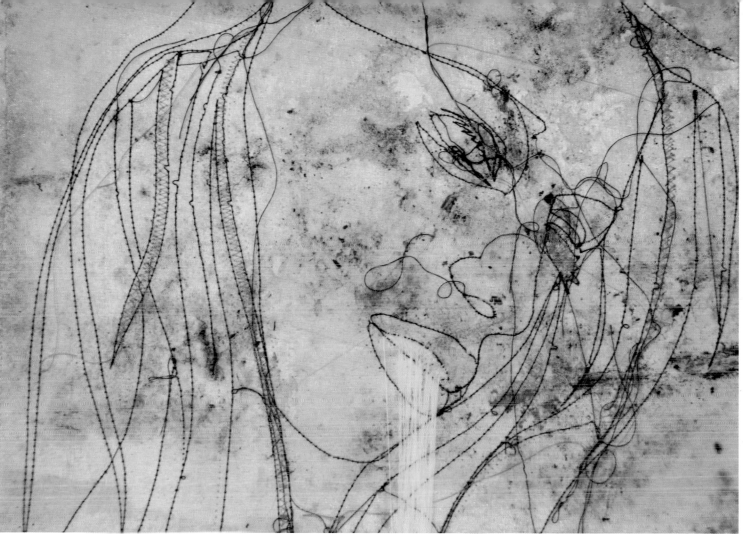

CLOCKWISE FROM FAR TOP LEFT:
LADY IN RED
Machine sewing, lace.

SURPRISE PARTY
Machine sewing onto transparent fabric and weathered watercolour paper.

BEAUTIFUL
Machine sewing onto transparent fabric and weathered watercolour paper.

NOTHINGNESS
Machine sewing onto transparent fabric and weathered watercolour paper.

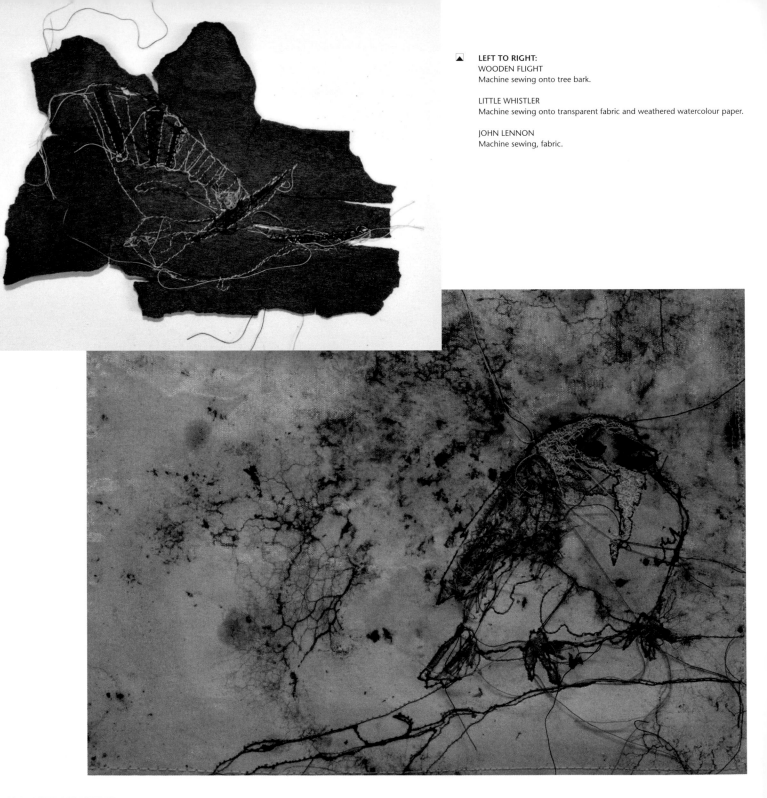

▲ **LEFT TO RIGHT:**
WOODEN FLIGHT
Machine sewing onto tree bark.

LITTLE WHISTLER
Machine sewing onto transparent fabric and weathered watercolour paper.

JOHN LENNON
Machine sewing, fabric.

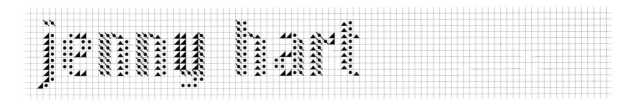

Jenny Hart

Jenny Hart is based in Austin, Texas, USA, and has been embroidering since 2000. She has always been a creative person with a passion for art and drawing, and is primarily a self-taught embroiderer. She explains:

I have a true obsession with embroidery. It's decorative embroidery applied to non-traditional themes. It's my drawing embellished with decorative stitches. It's portraiture, it's devotional, it represents a devotion of time and patience, it's embellishment as art. It's easier for me to say what it isn't! I do not describe my work as 'kitsch' or 'ironic' or necessarily 'feminist' (although I do acknowledge the relevance of the latter). I also do not consider myself a 'fibre artist' in the traditional sense, because I do not have any background or education in fibre arts, sewing or fabrics. I am an artist trained in traditional artistic disciplines (drawing, painting) and then adopted a medium that was completely foreign to me. I wanted to present it as something beautiful in a new way, worthy of being viewed as fine art. Embroidery is almost always secondary to a functional object and I wanted to use embroidery as the substance of my work itself.

Jenny has her own embroidery design company, Sublime Stitching, and has published several books of embroidery patterns and techniques for Chronicle Books. She has revolutionized embroidery by creating new and alternative designs, never before available, and has collaborated with other artists to produce designs based on their work. Her own preferred materials to work with are the simplest: plain cotton fabrics and cotton embroidery floss.

I do preparatory sketches, but only as a very basic starting point. I don't embroider practice pieces, but often I will abandon the embroidered version early on if I'm not happy with the direction it has taken. The majority of the composition is built gradually as I am doing the actual embroidery. I never work out the entire finished embroidered composition first, and a large part of the embroidery is free-form, worked directly on the fabric.

Jenny has exhibited her work widely in the United States and in France, and has also curated shows featuring other embroidery artists.

www.jennyhart.net
www.embroideryasart.com
www.feelingstitchy.com
www.sublimestitching.com

LEFT:
ALL THE GIRLS WEPT TEARS OF PURE LOVE/ST JOHN THE BAPTIST (JORDAN LEE)
Hand embroidery and sequins on cotton panel.
Included in a group show called 'Biblical Proportions' at Bearded Lady Gallery, Austin, Texas.

BELOW:
DOLLY PARTON
Hand embroidery on cotton.
Collection of Kevin Leonard, Chicago, Illinois.

LEFT TO RIGHT:

OH UNICORN
Artist's own hair embroidered
on leather.

IGGY POP
Hand embroidery on cotton.
'This piece was an open assignment
from *Nylon* magazine, where artists
were invited to create their "dream
bill concert poster" featuring any
line-up, at any venue, at any point
in history. I chose The Staple Singers
opening for Iggy Pop in the nursery
ward where I was born at the time
of my birth.'

DIRTY FACE, CROWNING GLORY
Hand embroidery on cotton.
Collection of Dan Ferrara, NYC.

◪ **LEFT TO RIGHT:**
CAVIAR
Crocheted lambswool, sequins, beads.

KATE'S CAFÉ
Crocheted lambswool.

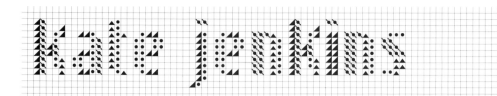

Kate Jenkins

Kate Jenkins is originally from Rhymney Valley, South Wales, but is now based in Brighton, England, where she launched her knitwear label and boutique Cardigan in 2003. Cardigan specializes in knitted, embroidered and crocheted accessories with 'a strong emphasis on colour and innovative, witty details'. It fulfils Kate's philosophy that 'anything can be created from yarn as long as it is made with love'.

Kate graduated from the University of Brighton with a BA in Fashion and Textiles in 1995. Immediately after graduating she became a freelance knitwear designer and worked for a number of well-known design companies. Overall, she has thirteen years' experience in the fashion and knitwear industry, designing for some of fashion's most prestigious designers including Donna Karan, Missoni and Sonia Rykiel.

Kate uses only crochet, taught to her by her mother and grandmother, for her artwork. She uses lambswool, adding sequins and beads as necessary. She explains:

The process is sometimes very quick and sometimes very time-consuming and slow, depending on the complexity of the design and whether I can achieve the way I want each piece to look. I sometimes sketch something out, but usually I start crocheting an idea straight away as I find it much easier – it's a bit like drawing with yarn. I try to find exact colours for yarn, sequins and beads every time I start a brand new piece of work, so it looks as believable as possible.

One of Kate's most popular projects is the 'Fish and Stitches' collection at Cardigan, which comprises food and culinary items reproduced as crocheted works of art. Everything from a plate of fish and chips to a tin of golden syrup has been lovingly recreated.

Kate's work has been exhibited at art fairs around the world including London, New York, Toronto, Paris and Amsterdam. Liberty of London asked Kate to create a small collection of framed insects based on her 2008 show entitled 'Cardigan in Bloom'. For this exhibition she 'celebrated nature in yarn and transformed her showroom into a magical garden where everything from the flowers to the tiny creatures nestling in the blooms was knitted and crocheted'.

In 2009 Kate had her first solo show, entitled 'Kate's Café', at The Rebecca Hossack Gallery in London. She transformed the gallery into a fantasy café all made from yarn. The show was received to high acclaim and was named 'show of the week' by the *Evening Standard*. The show was so successful that the gallery invited Kate back to do another show in 2010.

www.cardigan.ltd.uk

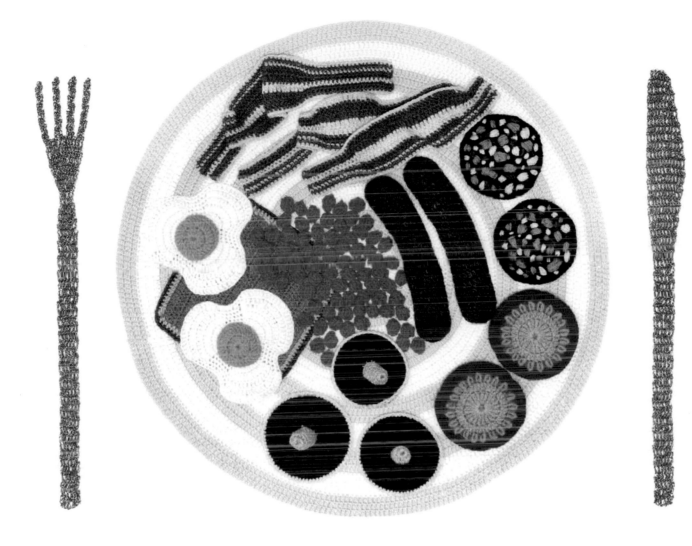

▲ **OPPOSITE, CLOCKWISE FROM TOP LEFT:**
SARDINE SALAD
Crocheted lambswool, sequins.

TAKEAWAY FISH AND CHIPS
Crocheted lambswool, sequins.

TINNED ANCHOVIES
Crocheted lambswool, sequins.

FISH AND CHIPS
Crocheted lambswool, sequins.

ABOVE:
FRIED BREAKFAST
Crocheted lambswool.

Knit the city

Knit the City is a group of yarnstormers from London, England, who followed in the footsteps of original US graffiti knitting collective Knitta Please. Knit the City's members are 'Agents of the Knit the City Yarn Corps': Deadly Knitshade, the Purple Purler, the Bluestocking Stitcher, Lady Loop, Shorn-a the Dead, Knitting Ninja and the Fastener.

Yarnstorming is another name for knitted graffiti where knitted items are left in public places. Knit the City use any kind of yarn they can get their hands on, as well as incorporating wire, pipe cleaners, buttons, sticks, fabric paints, soldering irons, felt, stuffing and, most recently, LEDs, batteries and bits of wire. They leave their knitted and crocheted mark on the streets of London:

Our yarnstorming tells the city's stories through its stitches. Each installation attempts to grab the passerby gently by the eyeballs and shove London and its history into their faces with a woolly squeal of delight/horror/humour.

Knit the City plan art installation projects together. Their most ambitious project to date has been their 'Oranges and Lemons Odyssey' in August 2009. They produced a knitted graffiti installation at six historic London churches mentioned in the 'Oranges and Lemons' nursery rhyme. It was installed over the course of one day, covering approximately eight miles (thirteen kilometres) between the churches. The event was covered live on Twitter over six hours and filmed by Alt Artist for a documentary. That wasn't the first time Knit the City have been filmed; they were featured on the BBC News website after a yarnstorm in Covent Garden, London.

www.knitthecity.com
www.bluestockingstitcher.wordpress.com – the Bluestocking Stitcher
www.ladyloop.wordpress.com – LadyLoop
www.thefastener.wordpress.com – the Fastener
www.thepurplepurler.com – the Purple Purler
www.whodunnknit.com – Deadly Knitshade

● **LEFT TO RIGHT:**
PHONE BOX COSY
A cover for a phone box in Parliament Square,
London. Knitting, crochet and embroidery with
yarn, cable ties.
'Police officers gave us a "stop and search" warning
during installation. One of them took a photo on
his phone afterwards for his wife.'

ORANGES AND LEMONS SERIES
Knitting, crochet and embroidery with yarn,
wire, bamboo, cotton, fabric pen, buttons,
beads and bells.

ST MARY LE BOW by the Bluestocking Stitcher

ST CLEMENT'S by the Purple Purler

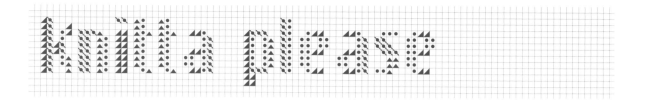

Knitta please

Knitta Please is the original knitted graffiti crew founded by Magda Sayeg, who is based in Austin, Texas, USA, and began knitting in her teens. The crew's 'yarnbombing' is their way of 'adding warmth' to their urban surroundings and their response to the homogenous mass production that surrounds us. Magda comments:

The goal I started with, and the goal that continues to drive me, is making this world more beautiful and interesting. But this ties into another element of my motivation: awareness of our urban environment; our urban furniture. My knit graffiti crafting started from a desire to make the steel and concrete urban world prettier. Although it's developed to be much more than that, this desire remains at the core of every project I do. It's about increasing the aesthetic value of our surroundings and initiating dialogue about art in public spaces and challenging the expectations of a passerby regarding what art can or should be.

Since the Knitta Please collective began in 2005, Magda has travelled all over the world tagging cities and taking part in commissioned projects and events. Knitta have been featured in numerous books and magazines and inspired countless people to take up their knitting needles and start up their own knit graffiti crews to brighten up their own urban environments.

Preparation for Knitta projects can vary, as Magda explains:

Once I find or dream up a project, I get the right dimensions for the objects I'm tagging and start knitting. I use stockinette stitch for all of my tags. To install the piece, I use either plastic zip ties or yarn or both to stitch up the seam. In the case of the Mexico City bus, I used liquid cement and repurposed afghans that I found at second-hand shops. In the beginning, I had to make practice pieces to figure out sizing and dimensions. Now, I sometimes make samples to test out colour swatches at the location. I use Photoshop to get an idea of the final design as well. I use any kind of yarn, as long as it is ridiculously bright – strong colours have a longer life in the sun/rain/weather.

Magda has many exciting plans for Knitta Please, including a collaborative book featuring examples of knitted graffiti from all over the world. Magda's dream projects would be to wrap a subway car and to tag an entire bridge. That would be no mean feat, but given all that this yarn revolutionary has achieved so far, we should keep our eyes on the Knitta Please website for any news.

www.knittaplease.com

◢ **LEFT TO RIGHT:**
MEXICO CITY BUS PROJECT
Acrylic yarn, repurposed
knitted and crocheted blankets,
plastic zip ties, liquid cement.
Photo: © Cesar Ortega.

SYDNEY OPERA HOUSE
Acrylic yarn and plastic zip ties.
Photo: © Daniel Fergus.

▲ **ABOVE:**
TRICOTEUSES
Knitta tag Paris for Bergère de France's 60th anniversary.
Wool yarn and plastic zip ties.
Photo: © Bergère de France.

ABOVE:
SYDNEY PEDESTRIAN SIGN
Acrylic yarn and plastic zip ties.
Photo: © Daniel Fergus.

RIGHT:
MONTAGUE ST, BROOKLYN
Magda Sayeg (right) and volunteer install a piece for 69 Meters,
Montague Street, Brooklyn.
Acrylic yarn and plastic zip ties.
Photo: © Jonathan Hokklo.

WE LOVE FASHION DOLLS
Hand-sewn and hand-embroidered fabrics, felt and beads.

DEER COLLAGE
Collage with paper, watercolour and felt.

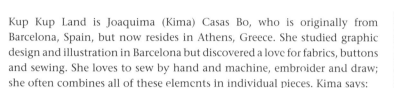Kup Kup land

Kup Kup Land is Joaquima (Kima) Casas Bo, who is originally from Barcelona, Spain, but now resides in Athens, Greece. She studied graphic design and illustration in Barcelona but discovered a love for fabrics, buttons and sewing. She loves to sew by hand and machine, embroider and draw; she often combines all of these elements in individual pieces. Kima says:

I started to play with fabrics, buttons, sewing, and I discovered felt: a fantastic material with which you can create a lot of things from illustration, and apply them to many interesting projects. I have always had a special interest in everything handmade. My style is kind of pop and baroque at the same time; I love to use many different colours and elements together. At times I try to make things more minimal – I really think that 'less is more', but in my work the results have never satisfied me so far.

Kup Kup Land is the name of the land where Kup Kup lives: Kup Kup is a little man who likes rambling around to find treasures. When I was searching for the name of the character I asked my son, who was three at the time, what he thought and he answered 'Kup Kup', which is what we call the small blanket that he has used to sleep with every day since he was a baby. I liked the name because it sounds nice and is something I can always share with my son.

Kima's favourite part of the creation process is turning the idea and design stage into something tangible. She always carries her Moleskine notebook with her so she can doodle whenever an idea strikes. Kima likes to experiment with different materials, but felt is a particular favourite; she likes to combine it with other materials such as wool and paper.

Kima has been involved in several exhibitions of her work in New York and San Francisco.

www.kupkup-land.blogspot.com
www.kupkup.etsy.com

LEFT TO RIGHT:
KUP KUP SCENERY
Hand-sewn and glued felt,
beads, wool, fabric and pins.

BIRD BROOCH
Hand-sewn fabric, felt and
wool.

DRESSED HORSE COLLAGE
Collage with paper and felt.

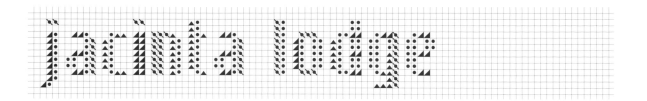

Jacinta Lodge

Jacinta Lodge is originally from Geelong, Australia, but is now based in Berlin, Germany. Embroidery is her main discipline, but she also practises cross stitch to relax. For the past nine years she has been concentrating on stumpwork, a form of embroidery where the design is raised from the fabric using wire, giving a 3D effect, and goldwork, another form of embroidery specifically using gold metal or other metallic threads.

Jacinta says she doesn't have a particular style, and that her style as well as her inspirations and influences are continually changing, although the pieces shown here were inspired by classic tattoo imagery:

I'm interested in pushing the techniques into new areas, not just depicting new, subversive or non-traditional images, but playing with the way in which the stitch is used. The tattoo-inspired stumpwork was obviously based on classic tattoo flash designs. My work since then has headed into more political territory, where I'm mostly interested in the way we train/indoctrinate our children to follow our own mindset. It's focusing more on the social aspects of belief. I'm also expanding my hand embroidery techniques to include fourteenth- to eighteenth-century styles. These I'm using in a way that evokes modern graffiti: the art of the protestor.

Jacinta didn't study textiles or embroidery formally; in fact, she has a degree in biochemistry, a doctorate in protein crystallography and in 2009 began a Master's in the regulation of pharmaceuticals. Her interest in embroidery started early on; it came from her mother, who was a textiles teacher and who taught Jacinta the basics of using a needle and thread.

Rather surprisingly, given the intricate nature of her work, Jacinta doesn't do a lot of planning or preparatory work before each piece:

It's rare that a piece is completely planned before I start. Technically I usually start from a few sketches, not too much planned out in detail. Then I just scrounge through my boxes until I find the threads or fabrics I want to use for it. I usually only buy threads specifically for a piece when I run out before the end, but I do stock up on a lot of speciality threads when I find them. I usually work on a stretcher bar frame, with the fabric also bound to the sides. Once the fabric is in place I'll just go for it, making up most of the details as I go along. The good thing about embroidery is that you can almost always unpick something you don't like.

www.stitchalicious.com

▲ **ALL IMAGES:**
MOTHER
Hand-embroidered stumpwork; satin,
embroidery floss, wire, felt.

Photos: Matti Hillig/foto di Matti,
www.foto-di-matti.com.

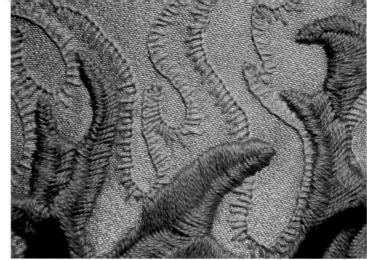

THIS PAGE:
BE CALM MY STITCHED AND FLAMING HEART
Hand-embroidered stumpwork;
satin, embroidery floss, wire, felt.

THIS PAGE:
AHOY
Hand-embroidered stumpwork; satin,
embroidery floss, felt, imitation leather,
passing threads, smooth purl.

Joetta maue

Joetta Maue is a full-time artist living and working in Brooklyn, New York. Joetta's work is inspired by and imbued with the everyday moments of her life. She is especially interested in the role of personal relationships in our lives, seen in our most intimate moments and spaces, and in exploring the conflicts and contradictions that exist there. She comments:

With my text work, I use language that comes from my everyday life, using phrases and words that relate and connect to the body, intimacy, romantic love and family. I am interested in how language can create connection and familiarity in the relationship between the viewer and me. I use my daily life as the main subject of my work; this inspiration comes from my feeling towards each daily moment and our everyday experience being the perfect moment, encouraging us to be present.

Prior to working in embroidery, Joetta mostly practised photography and printmaking, having gained a BFA in photography at Ohio State University and an MFA at the University of Massachusetts. Her embroidery still uses photography in the working process:

My image-based works all originate in a photograph. Through my photographic practice, for the last few years I have had the habit of documenting intimate moments with my husband, the little moments of quiet living and loving. These photographs are now translated into embroidered drawings. By taking the time to spend an hour embroidering my husband's nose or my own eyebrow, I am able to cherish and connect to the intimacy of love and companionship on a deeper level – and I hope this translates through the work to the viewer.

The role of craft practices such as embroidery and knitting are essential to Joetta's work because of their slow, meditative labour and their role in the history of the woman's voice. All of the linens used in her work are reappropriated, handmade or vintage linens that create a collaboration between her and women of the past. Joetta looks out for found vintage linens with pre-existing handwork, such as embroidery, lace work or tatting, at flea markets and antique stores that she can integrate into her work.

Her text and image work require slightly different preparation and processes:

I draw out all my designs on the fibre with a quilting pen, which allows me to follow the lines of the marker and keep shapes and lines straight. Text work is usually drawn directly on the fabric and worked on immediately without any changes. I generally do not have a plan in what colours I am going to use or what stitches; I just let the image unfold as a drawing would, responding to the shapes and memory of the image.

Joetta has exhibited her work widely throughout the United States. As well as maintaining her own websites, she contributes to www.hellocraft.com with articles focusing on contemporary artists working with craft techniques.

www.joettamaue.com
www.littleyellowbirds.blogspot.com

CLOCKWISE FROM RIGHT:
LINE
Outdoor installation at Governors Island, New York, hand-embroidered, appliquéd and cut reappropriated linens, homemade clothesline poles, clothesline, clothespins, trees, wind and sunshine.

EXHAUSTED
Hand-embroidered reappropriated linen, found linen with original embroidery, DMC thread.

BREAKS MY HEART…
Hand-embroidered reappropriated linen, found linen with original embroidery, DMC thread.

TOUCH
Hand-embroidered reappropriated linens, found set of pillowcases with original embroidery, DMC thread, cotton fabric, acrylic paint, shelf.

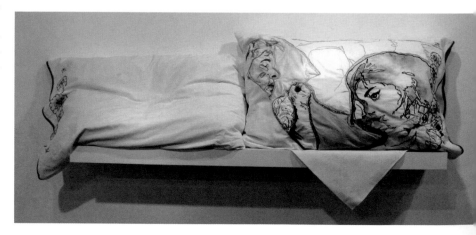

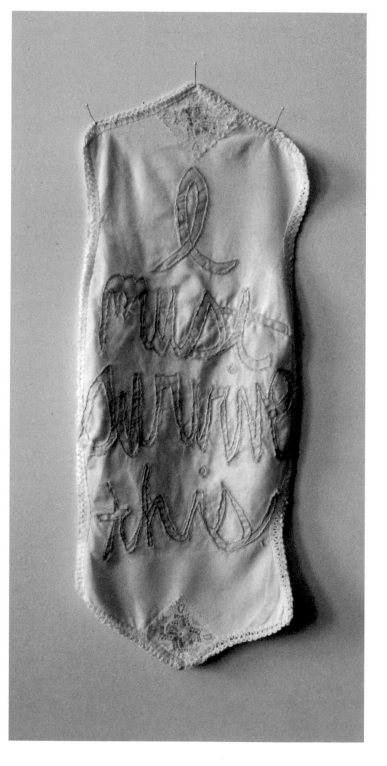

LEFT:
IN WORKING THOUGHT
Hand-embroidered
reappropriated linen, found
linen with original embroidery,
DMC thread, found wood
hanger, embroidery hoop.

OPPOSITE, CLOCKWISE FROM TOP LEFT:
AFRAID YOU WILL STOP
Hand-embroidered reappropriated linen, found handkerchief, DMC thread, wooden embroidery hoop.

MUST SURVIVE
Hand-appliquéd reappropriated linen, found linen with original embroidery, DMC thread, found cotton fabric.

FUCKED UP AND FLAWED
Hand-embroidered reappropriated linen, found linen with original handwork, DMC thread.

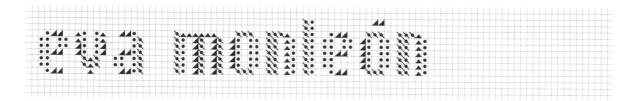

eva monleón

Eva Monleón, from Barcelona, Spain, works under the pseudonym Misako Mimoko. She creates plush character dolls: Dolis for female dolls, Dolos for male dolls. Eva describes her work as:

one-of-a-kind handmade dolls or stuffed toys for grown-ups with a careful vintage and kawaii aesthetic [cute with an intriguing or vulnerable side], and naïve handmade finishing. I create these handmade dolls as kitsch objects. It isn't neo-kitsch, based on bad taste or camp, but kitsch that appeared in the middle of the nineteenth century, when a deep feeling of loss and nostalgia for pre-industrial objects and nature arose.

Eva learned embroidery, needlepoint, cross stitch and crochet at primary school and went on to study Fine Arts at the University of Barcelona. She began making her dolls in 2008 as an outlet for her love of craft and as a break from her day job as a designer, working with computers. Eva's inspirations for forms and characters can come from anywhere, and she sources her materials from flea markets, charity or second-hand shops. Her approach and process of creation is unstructured and spontaneous, like many of the artist–makers featured in this book. She explains:

I create a new doll from anything; it can be from an animal, an object or a plant that I'd like to see as a doll, then I draw a sketch. At the beginning I used a computer to make the pattern and test colours, but now I draw the pattern directly on paper. Then I choose fabrics carefully and put colours together. I love playing. I'm completely smitten with all kinds of fabric, but especially linen and wool. I adore natural and colourful yarns, vintage laces, ribbons and trims. I always look for a whimsical and vintage look. I sew all the different parts of the body separately by machine, then I stuff each piece (very hard) with polyfill and hand stitch one to another to make the body. Embroidering the little face is the last part of the process. I love to adorn the dolls with outrageous bows and laces, crocheted or felted accessories. I always work on the final piece, enjoying the fact that when I start making a new creation I never know

how it will come out. I just let her or him appear. I love to make mistakes, imperfections, darns and mends. I go back many times, unpicking. Each piece has its own life and story. Since we aren't perfect, my dolls aren't either. I try making them look like old second-hand toys: worn and a little scruffy from being loved, mended by rough hands, thereby stamping my mark and personal traces.

www.misakomimoko.com
www.misakomimoko.blogspot.com

CLOCKWISE FROM BELOW:
THE FRIENDLY GHOST NECKLACE
Plush, hand embroidery, jewellery, painting, machine sewing and hand sewing; chain, acrylic paint, cotton, felt and polyfill.

DOLI LITTLE DONKEY EARS
Amigurumi, plush, hand embroidery, machine sewing and hand sewing; linen, cotton, ribbon, felt, golden embroidery thread, yarn and polyfill.

DOLO CROISSANT
Crochet, plush, hand embroidery, machine sewing and hand sewing; linen, cotton, felt, wool, yarn and polyfill.

THIS PAGE, CLOCKWISE FROM ABOVE:
DOLI LITTLE BANK ROBBER
Crochet, plush, hand embroidery, machine and hand sewing; linen, cotton, ribbon, elastic band, plush, yarn and polyfill.

A NICE COUPLE: DOLO CROISSANT AND DOLI PINK MERINGUE
Crochet, plush, hand embroidery, machine and hand sewing; linen, cotton, felt, wool, yarn, ribbon and polyfill.

DOLIS Y DOLOS LITTLE FRIENDS
Crochet, plush, hand embroidery, machine and hand sewing; linen, cotton, ribbon, yarn, felt, synthetic leather, pin and polyfill.

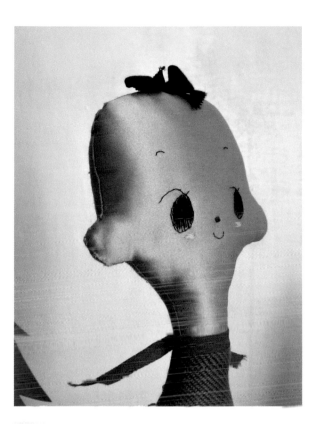

▲ **THIS PAGE, CLOCKWISE FROM ABOVE:**
DOLI DOGGY
Crochet, plush, hand embroidery, machine and hand sewing; cotton,
ribbon, felt, yarn and polyfill.

DOLI LITTLE MERMAID
Plush, hand embroidery, machine and hand sewing; linen, cotton, ribbon,
felt, plush and polyfill.

DOLI LITTLE LIGHT BULB
Plush, hand embroidery, machine and hand sewing; cotton, linen, felt,
ribbon and polyfill.

■ DOLI BUNNY
Plush, hand embroidery, machine and hand sewing;
linen, cotton, ribbon, felt and polyfill.

LEFT:
THE FRIENDLY GHOST
Plush, hand embroidery, painting, stamping, machine and hand sewing; pin, wood, bakery twine, stamping ink, acrylic paint, cotton, felt and polyfill.

BELOW:
DOLI LITTLE LIONESS, back detail.
Crochet, plush, hand embroidery, machine and hand sewing; linen, cotton, tulle, felt, pipe cleaner, yarn and polyfill.

ABOVE:
CANDY?
Wool fibre.
'This piece combines my love
of replica and naughtiness.'

RIGHT:
UNTITLED
Wool fibre.
'You can't see it in the photo,
but there is a little red felted
"ember" on the tip of the
ciggie.'

OPPOSITE:
APOCA-GALÁPAGOS SERIES,
SPECIMEN 1
Wool fibre, doll head.

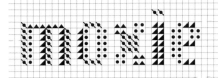

Moxie was born in New York, raised in Northern California and has been based in Seattle for eleven years.

She originally studied graphic design, but decided not to pursue it as a career. For the last five years she has been working primarily in the discipline of needle felting. Moxie has been making things with her hands for as long as she can remember, but when she learned to needle felt she 'pretty much stopped doing everything else'. She comments:

Needle felting allows me to communicate through fibre alchemy, revelling in the transformation of soft, comforting wool fibre into art objects that are solid to the touch. My work uses no water, knitting, sewing, stuffing or embroidery: I sculpt using only my hands, wool fibre, industrial felting needles and time. This is part of what is so unique about my work: I manage to do everything without additional tools or techniques. It's a little OCD, but I love the results I get!

Needle felting is an incredibly labour-intensive art form. Moxie's recreation of the Fisher Price dog as a large sculpture, for example, took upwards of forty hours to complete.

Most often, I start with an idea in my mind, and then do rough sketches if I have trouble executing shapes or design. For replicas, I reference the real items or photographs to be as accurate as possible. I almost never start out intending to make a 'prototype', but I definitely learn during the process and will discard a piece to start again if I've discovered a better way to get where I want to go. I believe uncertainty is part of the process.

Moxie mostly works with Corriedale wool, but loves all kinds of fibre. She also often combines her needle felting with found objects:

I'm constantly distracted by discarded plastic pieces on the sidewalk, broken toys at garage sales, or thrift store collectibles that need rescuing. I often don't know what these collected treasures will become, only that there is an inherent potential in the things I gather.

www.madebymoxie.com

THIS PAGE, CLOCKWISE FROM LEFT:

RESISTOR
Wool fibre, wire armature.
'A replica inspired by electric components. The grey extensions are felted around a wire armature so they can be bent like the real thing.'

NOT FOOD
Wool fibre.
'A Salisbury steak TV dinner is absolutely not food... and neither is this sculpture. Each little pea and the steak itself are felted separately, but the disturbingly accurate mashed potatoes and the brownie dessert are felted right into the tray.'

PLANS
Wool fibre.
'Two finger puppets when put together create a story... to me it's about best friends and bad intentions.'

● **ABOVE LEFT:**
FRIENDS
Wool fibre.
'Puppets need puppets too.'

ABOVE RIGHT:
UNTITLED
Wool fibre.
'This was my first large-scale sculpture. The Fisher Price Little People were
a big part of my childhood and I wanted to explore the iconic shape of
this dog. By the way, it weighs three pounds.'

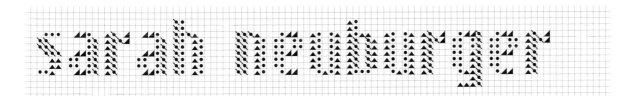

sarah neuburger

Sarah Neuburger is based in Savannah, Georgia, USA, and has been crafting her whole life:

My family is very industrious; we all have a wide variety of interests and a deep desire to understand how things work and how they are made, so we've made things since day one. I always had handmade clothing growing up. I learned to cross stitch by the end of grade school; I learned to sew and read patterns by the end of middle school, and took my first wood shop class about the same time.

Sarah turned her crafty industrious nature into her business, The Small Object, six years ago. She sells a variety of 'Small Objects', including her clothespin peg dolls in a variety of forms from custom-made keepsakes such as wedding cake toppers, to cupcake topper candle-holders, finger puppets and 'wooden hanger pals'. She also creates stationery items including stickers and rubber stamps with her trademark simple happy-faced line drawings.

Sarah's work is very much inspired and influenced by personal nostalgia; her 'Home Sweet Home' stamp is inspired by a drawing of a house she made when she was just five years old, and her wooden cupcake topper (a wooden doll with the cake as a skirt) was inspired by a popular cake design that her mother made for her sister's sixth birthday.

Sarah uses paints, pens and pencils to create her pieces and sources other materials from just about anywhere: eBay, Etsy, thrift stores, fabric stores and quilt shops. She comments:

For me, often the technique will dictate what type of process I use to create the image. For my shop, most of the pieces are about putting my image or drawing onto an everyday item that you use in your home or craft-making. Quite often, I make several pages of drawings, then scan them into my computer to do final small changes before either making a screen for printing or sending them out-of-house for stationery printing or for the ways I have found to put my drawings onto various objects. For the handmade wooden wedding toppers, the wooden peg dolls are all individually constructed using a clothespin base. I have created patterns for their clothing and have lots of small flowers, ribbons and millinery bits for their accessories. For those, I do not sketch out ideas first but will be inspired by a piece of vintage ribbon or by the colours of my clients' weddings. I place a number of items on the piece and try them in different configurations before securing them all together.

Sarah and her work have been featured in several books, while gift books and journals featuring her designs have been produced by Chronicle Books. She was also featured in the book and documentary *Handmade Nation*.

www.thesmallobject.com
www.togetherforever.etsy.com

OPPOSITE, CLOCKWISE FROM LEFT:
CELEBRATION CANDLE KID
Cake topper and candle-holder, wood, paint, fabric.

PENELOPE PICNIC
Wood, fabric, paint, multi-media.

CUSTOM WEDDING CAKE TOPPER
Wood, fabric, paint, multi-media.

ABOVE:
CUSTOM WEDDING CAKE TOPPER DETAIL
Wood, fabric, paint, multi-media.

SARAH NEUBURGER • 079

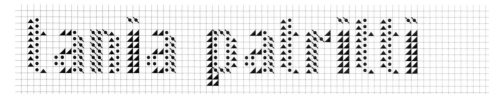

tania patritti

Tania Patritti sells her homemade stuffed characters under the name Ninon. She is originally from a little town in the Alps in northern Italy, but since 2007 she has lived in Berlin, Germany. Tania says:

I started sewing in 2001 and making my Les Monstris in 2004 – characters that are colourful and a bit weird. I think that they are cute but also disturbing at the same time. I like to invent creatures that don't exist!

Tania's inspiration comes from a strong connection to her own childhood and to childhood in general. She was taught to use a sewing machine by her mother and taught herself the rest. Her formal higher education was in art history. Her process and technique is very fluid:

I never make patterns; every piece I make is one of a kind. Sometimes the final idea comes from a drawing, but more often it's a combination of elements taken from different sketches. I usually cut directly on the fabric, after choosing the combination of patterns and colours of it. The part of the work that I like best is making the face: choosing the position of the different facial features and expression. This is the most important part! Lately I've been working on the freehand machine embroidery technique: it's like using the needle as if it were a pencil, and it's very interesting because it makes the results even more unique and not reproducible.

As a self-confessed fabric addict, Tania collects fabric everywhere she goes – thrift shops, flea markets and fabric stores. Tania has exhibited her creations widely in Europe, the United States and Japan.

www.ninon.etsy.com
www.superninon.blogspot.com

CLOCKWISE FROM BELOW:
BUBS MAHONEY
Stuffed monster made with
faux fur, cotton, buttons, felt
and polyfill.

ONE OF THE PIROLETTI
BROTHERS
Faux fur, felt, buttons and
polyfill.

THE WILD BUNCH
Mixed fabric, felt, faux fur,
buttons and polyfill.

CLOCKWISE FROM ABOVE:
SOUP JOHN MANCHEWSKI
Stuffed monster made with linen, cotton, faux fur, buttons and polyfill.

NEIGHBOURS
Group of monsters meeting on the staircase; mixed fabric, felt, faux fur and polyfill.

GASPARD E. PINOPINE
Stuffed creature made with faux fur, linen, felt, cotton, buttons and polyfill.

THE CHERRYBOMB FAMILY
Mixed fabric, polyfill and hand sewing.

BUDDIES HANGIN' OUT
Group of dolls and monsters; mixed fabric, felt, faux fur and polyfill.

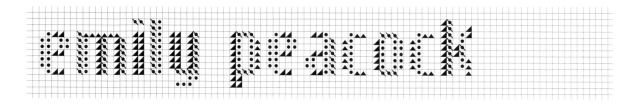

emily peacock

Emily Peacock is based in Marlow, Buckinghamshire, England. She started her business producing needlepoint kits of her own designs in 2007. She describes her work as a fresh take on traditional tapestry:

I produce designs that would look 'at home' in modern or traditional settings. My ideas are drawn from my surroundings as well as from how I feel about my life. The themes change, but I try to make my designs upbeat and colourful. I love to use typefaces and this can give the work a certain romantic, nostalgic feel.

Emily has been stitching since she was old enough to control a needle. She has always had craft projects on the go, finding it relaxing and therapeutic. She began working on her own designs when she moved with her family to the southwest of France.

It was a difficult time and I felt quite lost in a very different culture. I needed craft to ground me and this was the perfect opportunity to explore my own talents. I was always frustrated by the designs available on the market and I wondered why traditional craft had to mean traditional designs. There was nothing new or vibrant about what I saw, so I created my own.

Emily has worked in graphic and typesetting studios, thereby gaining an understanding of design, colour and type. She always hand-draws her ideas first and at the last stage she uses computer software to produce a chart. She comments:

A lot of cross stitch designs on the market today look as if they have been scanned in at the outset from a photo, and I believe this compromises the personality of a design. I use cross stitch on canvas worked from a colour chart. I use a blank canvas because I think it is far more enjoyable to watch the design grow, as if you are painting with the stitches, rather than stitch over a pre-printed canvas. Most tapestry kits available on the market use tent stitch. I prefer cross stitch, however, as lines

and shapes within the design are bolder. Tent stitch gives a diagonal look to a design, as it is a diagonal stitch. It almost looks as if the design is in the rain! Another benefit of cross stitch is that it doesn't distort the canvas in the way that tent stitch does. Cross stitch is worked in two directions, which leaves the canvas square. I prefer to work from a chart, as it is more accurate; this is important when stitching lettering.

Emily uses high-quality materials for her kits: Appleton wools on Zweigart canvas. She loves to work in wool for the softness it brings to a room. Emily is a regular contributor to *Cross Stitcher* magazine.

www.emilypeacock.com

CLOCKWISE FROM BELOW:
RODEO
CORDELIA
STARS OVER CORN
IN BLOOM
PRIMAL SUN

CLOCKWISE FROM RIGHT:
KISS
HUG
FAITH
LOVE
TAKING FLIGHT
HOPE

▲ **THIS PAGE FROM LEFT:**
All works are hand-crochet, mohair wool, and reproduction animal parts.
Photos: Scenephotography.co.uk.

STAG
URBAN STAG

OPPOSITE:
RUNNING HARE

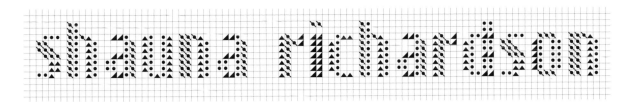

shauna richardson

Shauna Richardson is originally from Northern Ireland and is based in Leicester, England, where she practises her 'crochetdermy' – crocheted versions of taxidermy animals, inspired by examples of Victorian taxidermy. She learned to crochet at school aged nine and went on to study Fine Art at De Montfort University, Leicester, in 2001.

Shauna sources her materials from all over the world. Her process for creating her pieces is very spontaneous and free-form; she doesn't create or work from any patterns. She explains:

Using one colour and one stitch, I freestyle crochet directly onto to the life-size form, tracing anatomical detail, bone structure and muscle definition as I go creating the beast's 'skin'. If you were able to remove the form from a completed sculpture, the crochet 'skin' would be in one, single piece. I use high-quality materials: the yarn is mohair wool, the eyes are glass, and the antlers, jaws, teeth and claws are reproduction. No animal is harmed in the production!

Shauna was one of twelve artists given the opportunity to create a project for the UK's 2012 Cultural Olympiad, representing the East Midlands. Her project is 'Lionheart' – three crocheted thirty-foot lions to be displayed in a glass case in Nottingham. The inspiration for the project is Richard the Lionheart, while the wool material represents the region's textile industry. She comments:

I have been crocheting all my life and have long been a conceptual artist, but not until comparatively recently did I begin to combine the two. Traditional craft and realism – areas largely avoided in contemporary art – are celebrated in my work. I create large unique animal sculptures that blur the boundaries between craft and art, prompt dialogue and promote traditional craft as a valid contemporary medium. Naturally drawn to the world of curiosity, I take inspiration from Victorian taxidermy and travelling menageries in order to create my own 'uncanny' beast show. The animal form generates immediate impact.*

On closer inspection, the stitches reveal themselves and the crochet quietly grows in magnitude, taking on a life of its own. Crochet is a skill practised worldwide and is accessible to all. I aim to delight and ignite the imagination, challenge preconceptions and breathe new life into traditional craft skills.

www.shaunarichardson.com

* Uncanny (German, *unheimliche* – literally, 'unhomely') is a Freudian concept of an instance where something can be familiar yet foreign at the same time, resulting in a feeling of it being uncomfortably strange.

LEFT TO RIGHT:
All works are hand-crochet, mohair wool, and reproduction animal parts.
Photos: Scenephotography.co.uk.

BROWN BEAR
FOX
HARE

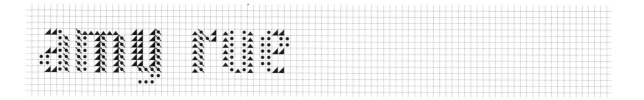

amy rue

Amy Rue is based in Jasper, Georgia, USA, where she creates her 'Lumplings' – handmade, one-of-a-kind rag dolls. She is completely self-taught and 'makes it all up as she goes along'. She explains:

The Lumplings are lumpy, bumpy and never perfect, which is just how I love them. They are usually between eight and eleven inches tall and like to travel in small herds. They come together in a few different ways: I scrounge through my fabric stash and come up with colours and patterns that make me happy and then I draw my Lumpling shape directly on the fabric. I stitch around that drawn line, trim, turn it inside out, stuff and the face is done last. The shape tells me the personality that the face must have; that is why I do it last. I usually sew the body together with a sewing machine; the face I do by hand. My children inspire a lot of what I do; they suggest Lumpling names, shapes and stories to me.

Amy was inspired as a child by the *Little House on the Prairie* books and how Laura Ingalls had a handmade rag doll called Charlotte. Amy is also inspired by the Beatrix Potter stories her granny read to her, and the personalities Potter gave to the animals.

Amy's Lumplings are made from heirloom-quality mohair, pure cashmere, wool, cotton or soft minky and have vintage button eyes. She comments:

Steiff animals are the reason I wanted to work with mohair, which also came from my granny, as she has always collected old bears and anything Steiff. We have family outings to thrift stores looking for cashmere and wool sweaters. I also use eBay, while I buy mohair and minky from online retailers.

As well as sewing Lumpling rag dolls, Amy also practises photography and paints with acrylics and watercolour. Her paintings sometimes involve collage with photos and found objects.

Amy's Lumplings were used in the film *Mr Magorium's Wonder Emporium* (2007) for the toy store scenes.

www.amyrue.com
www.amyrue.etsy.com

LEFT TO RIGHT:
YOM-YOM BUNNY LUMPLING
Mohair, stuffing, buttons, hand stitching.

RUMPY AND PUMPY CAT AND HER BABY BUNNY LUMPLINGS
Mohair, stuffing, buttons, hand stitching.

WHITE BUNNY LUMPLING WITH APPLE
Mohair, corduroy, stuffing, buttons, hand stitching.

Rumpy
&
Pumpy
amyrue.com

CLOCKWISE FROM LEFT:
STRIPED KITTY LUMPLING
Cashmere, stuffing, buttons, hand stitching.

PINK BUNNY LUMPLING DETAIL
Mohair, stuffing, buttons, hand stitching.

BEAR LUMPLING AND WREATH
Mohair, stuffing, buttons, hand stitching.

LEFT:
BABY BROW CAT LUMPLING
Wool, buttons, stuffing, hand stitching.

ABOVE:
BROWN BUNNY LUMPLING WITH APPLE
Mohair, stuffing, buttons, hand stitching.

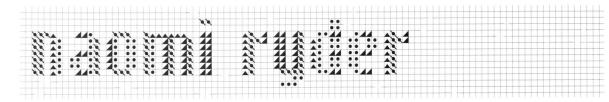

naomi ryder

Naomi Ryder is a textile designer and illustrator born in Leicester, England, but who now lives and works in London. Her main discipline is both hand and freehand machine embroidery. She also combines the traditional craft of embroidery with digital and screenprinting techniques. She explains:

I specialize in embroidery: drawing with stitches to create beautiful images of the everyday. I combine my love of drawing with textile work, using both hand and machine embroidery and occasionally using print. I embroider bespoke silk chiffon curtains, create artwork pieces and from this design interior products such as tea towels, cushions and lavender bags. I am currently developing wallpaper and porcelain collections.

Naomi's grandmother taught her how to knit and sew, and she went on to study embroidery at Manchester Metropolitan University from 1991 to 1994. Naomi always uses photographs as the inspiration and starting point of her work:

I am always photographing for inspiration. I then sketch or photograph the subject matter I like to use. I always make a sketch; it is vital to my work to get the initial drawings right. I need a clear drawing and then apply this to the fabric. I use an embroidery hoop and stitch the images using a domestic sewing machine. For my patterns I place the images in Photoshop and create patterns that I can print digitally onto fabric or on paper.

Naomi loves working with natural fibres such as felted wools, cotton, velvets and silk. Some of her pieces are naturally dyed, while for small sections of appliqué she often uses vintage fabrics, which she usually sources from charity or thrift shops, utilizing old clothes or pieces of tablecloths. She buys the silks and wools she uses new from all over the world, in order to get the right 'luxury quality' she needs for her pieces.

Naomi has taken part in group and solo exhibitions, worked on commissions for Domino records and Habitat, provided illustrations for magazines, and worked with well-known fashion designers. She adds:

My main source of inspiration is the beauty and humour found in the day-to-day, mundane, routine tasks that make up our daily lives. I have explored this theme by stitching people brushing their teeth, getting out of bed and talking on the telephone. I present such ordinary moments using delicate and luxury materials that create an interesting contrast between essential and superfluous, beauty and ordinary.

www.naomiryder.co.uk

CLOCKWISE FROM FAR LEFT:
MARK TUCKS HIS SHIRT IN
Embroidery on fine cream,
wool fabric curtain.

AMY
Freehand machine embroidery
on a silk chiffon curtain.

THURSTON
Embroidery onto naturally dyed
silk, for *Plan B* magazine.

NATIONAL GALLERY
Silk chiffon curtains were
embroidered with ten galleries
of London for the Queen
Elizabeth Hall on London's
South Bank.

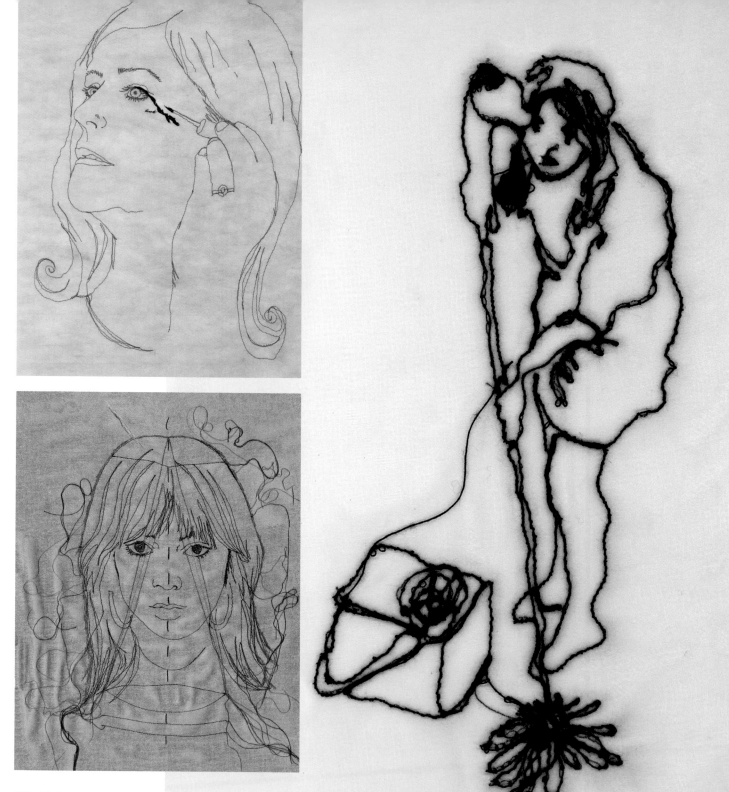

CLOCKWISE FROM FAR TOP LEFT:

DON'T APPLY YOUR EYELINER ON THE TRAIN
From the series of three 'Unfortunate Incidents', embroidered onto naturally dyed silk duchess. Freehand machine embroidery and hand stitching for the eyes.

MOPPING
One of forty illustrations embroidered onto silk chiffon.
'This is the day in the life of my friend Katherine. I followed her around for a day sketching her doing ordinary things and tried to make them into something beautiful.'

CAT POWER PORTRAIT
Freehand machine embroidery on acid yellow fabric, for an Irish magazine.

TAXI
Embroidered detail on a silk chiffon curtain with forms of London transport.

CHROMATICS
A poster for the band Chromatics, embroidery on naturally dyed fabric.

William Schaff

William Schaff is based in Warren, Rhode Island, USA, and partakes in embroidery, paper cutting, drawing, collage, painting and dioramas. He has been embroidering for about six years and initially started when he felt that he and his girlfriend had been watching too much TV:

I had gotten my gal the entire series of The X-Files *on DVD, and before you know it I realized we were spending seven to eight hours a day watching television! Feeling remiss in my duties, I remembered I had always wanted to try embroidery. I figured it was something I could do while watching TV. Thus a joy with embroidery was born!*

William studied classical figure studies at the Maryland Institute College of Art, in Baltimore. He didn't formally study textile art; his interest in embroidery came much later, when he taught himself by looking at other people's work. He approaches his embroidery work as if he is drawing with the needle and floss, unconcerned about learning formal or traditional techniques:

It is fairly straightforward, and probably not very true to the tradition of this particular craft. I simply sketch out what I will be working on onto the fabric. From there, I choose my threads and dive in. I usually start around the face, more out of habit than for any artistic reason. I really just look at each stitch as a pencil mark, trying to figure out which direction it should go in, and what colour it should be.

William's inspirations and subject matter vary greatly. His commercial projects have seen him produce work for independent musicians such as Okkervil River and Godspeed You! Black Emperor.

It's funny, I go from two extremes – biblical characters, which I guess would be very traditional, to those things normally found in my work: observations of how people interact in the world. I also do a series of patches for this renegade brass band from around here, The What Cheer? Brigade. It's fun because each member picks something special to them, and I run with it.

www.williamschaff.com
www.whatcheerbrigade.com

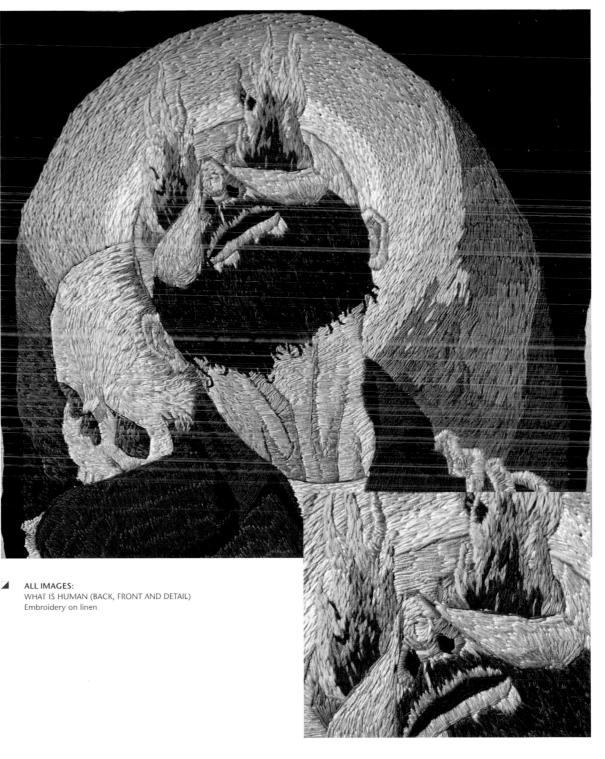

◢ **ALL IMAGES:**
WHAT IS HUMAN (BACK, FRONT AND DETAIL)
Embroidery on linen.

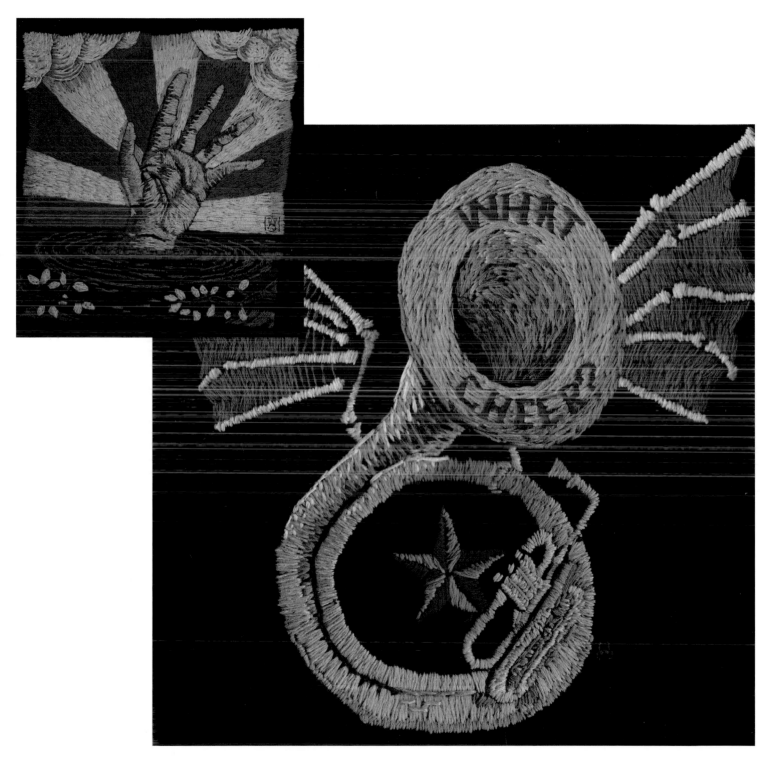

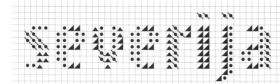

severija

Severija Inčirauskaité-Kriaunevičiené was born in Vilnius, Lithuania. She studied textile art at the Vilnius Academy of Fine Arts, where she was awarded a Master's degree.

Severija is a highly regarded contemporary gallery artist and has been invited to install her award-winning work widely in solo and group shows throughout Europe and the UK. Although Severija essentially uses the technique of cross stitching to create her work, she juxtaposes this textile-based discipline with working with the unexpected material of metal, drilled to create holes for cross stitching. She has worked with all sorts of metal items, from car doors to soup ladles to watering cans. She comments:

In my work, I take pleasure in things that are only insignificant details to most people. An ordinary human being and mundane fragments of his or her life acquire an exceptionally important meaning in my works; meanwhile, recognized icons of beauty are less important to me. A banal understanding of beauty and utilitarian things: these are the objects that interest me and inspire creation. Therefore, I use fragments of popular culture, the so-called kitsch, in my art. When they appear in a new context, like some kind of 'quotation', they help to create works that reveal my personal experience and point of view. Today the archaic cross stitching technique reminds us of not very tasteful, stereotype, 'philistine' embroideries. By choosing it and quite 'syrupy' kitsch fragments of popular culture and transforming them into aesthetic objects of textile, I raise doubt in the traditional hierarchy of art, between what is usually called 'high art' and less valuable art. In my works, the kitsch details of popular culture lose their clearly negative contents. A simple understanding of beauty characteristic to ordinary people can also be valuable at least, because it is part of life and sincere.

www.severija.lt

CLOCKWISE FROM RIGHT:
OBJECT OF COMPARISON (two images)
Iron details, cotton, cross stitch, drilling.

DIRECTION
Metal shovel, cotton, cross stitch, drilling.

ONCE UPON A TIME IN THE SOUP
Metal spoon, cotton, cross stitch, drilling.

FAR LEFT:
WAY OF ROSES
Installation from the project 'Art In Unusual Places',
initiated by Vilnius European Capital of Culture 2009.

CENTRE:
AUTUMN COLLECTION
Old rusted metal things, cotton, cross stitch, drilling.

THIS PAGE:
BETWEEN CITY AND VILLAGE
Metal pail, watering can, cotton, cross stitch, drilling.

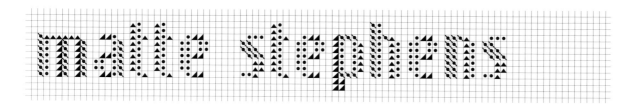

matte stephens

Matte Stephens is a self-taught artist. He is originally from Alabama but now lives in Portland, Oregon, with his wife and fellow artist and contributor Vivienne Strauss.

Matte is predominantly a painter and illustrator and has produced work commercially for many companies and magazines. Matte's felt characters are made using the needle-felt sculpting technique, where pieces of felt are sculpted into shape using barbed needles. He describes his work as happy, and his characters are all based on characters and images from his paintings.

I am primarily a painter but also enjoy working with wool felt and making paper sculptures. I started working in felt when I needed to take breaks from painting. All of my felted animals were inspired by paintings I had done previously.

Matte loves mid-twentieth-century industrial and graphic design, for instance the work of Charles and Ray Eames and Alexander Girard, as well as fine artists of the same era such as Ben Shahn and Paul Klee.

www.matteart.net
matteart.blogspot.com

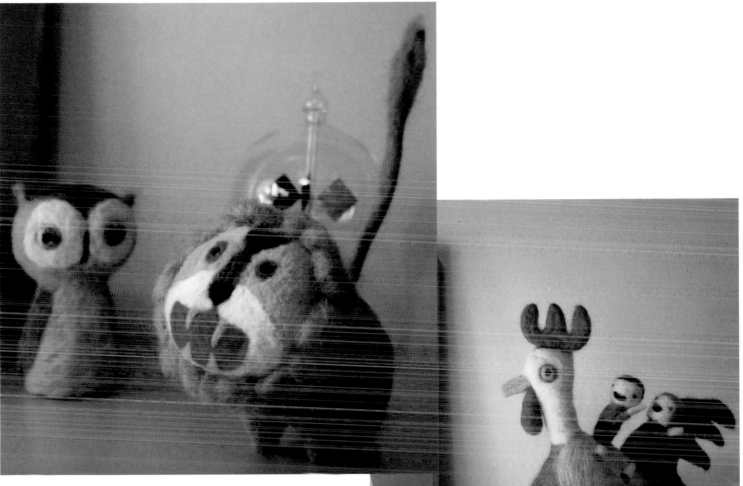

LEFT TO RIGHT:
All items are needle-felted figures.

MR OWL AND HIS MOTHER
MR OWL AND UNCLE RUTHERFORD
AUGUSTUS THE LION FELTED FELLOW
FELTED ROOSTER SCHOOL BUS AND MR OWL

▲

CLOCKWISE FROM BELOW:
DARIA TAKES BEAUMONT FOR A WALK
Hand embroidery and appliqué on unbleached muslin.

ANTOINE DOES HIS BEST TO IMPRESS BABETTE
Hand embroidery, appliquéd on linen.

ESTHER'S SOCIAL LIFE HAD DWINDLED DOWN TO NIL SINCE ALL SHE WANTED TO TALK ABOUT WERE HER DACHSHUNDS
Hand embroidery on linen.

vivienne strauss

Vivienne Strauss is a full-time artist living in Portland, Oregon, with her husband, fellow artist and contributor Matte Stephens. She has a degree in philosophy but no formal training in the arts. Vivienne is primarily a painter working in watercolour and acrylics, and works with collage as well as embroidery. She says:

I love the process of hand stitching, though I am the worst seamstress ever, but with embroidery I can create with thread and not be concerned about proper measurements. I'm completely self-taught and although I have referred to various books for technique, I'm really bad about imposing all kinds of 'rules' on myself while I work and have to constantly remind myself that there really aren't any rules and I can do as I please.

For her embroidery work Vivienne prefers to work with cotton or linen and sometimes with vintage fabric. She has recently experimented with working on a felted wool panel and plans to work with it more in the future.

I like to work with a colourful palette when I paint or embroider. I keep the work on the light and whimsical side, and I like to make people laugh! I am primarily inspired by classic and foreign films, but also by phrases I find in books that I read. Often I'm inspired by a particular image (an old photo or a scene from a film) but then when I'm painting or embroidering, a new story evolves as I work. I start out with a rough sketch, but I don't draw anything out on the fabric; once I start stitching, I don't like to be confined by anything, I would rather let the work develop on its own.

Vivienne has exhibited her work across the United States and in Japan.

www.vivienneart.blogspot.com
www.vivstrauss.etsy.com

• **RIGHT:**
PABLO TRAVELS THE WORLD IN SEARCH OF HOPE
Hand embroidery, appliquéd on unbleached muslin.

THIS PAGE, CLOCKWISE FROM LEFT
All pieces made by crochet,
sewing and embroidery using yarn,
polyester fibrefill and glass eyes.

HUNGRY LIKE THE WOOFGANG
A LESSON IN SHARING
DON'T MESS WITH DIABLO

OPPOSITE:
REX OF THE CARROT-CIDALS

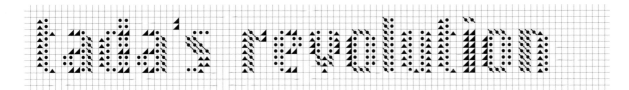

tada's revolution

Tada's Revolution, based in St Louis, Missouri, are Susan Chi (characters, art direction, photography) and Nicholas Nguyen (set/prop design, art direction, photography). Susan named her collection of work after Tada – a very tattered bear that she bought on eBay. On her website she explains:

I decided to name my collection of work after Tada because it has grown to share much in common with the Tada experience. Tada's Revolution is rebirth. It represents redemption from the garbage pile; it represents salvation from an otherwise ordinary, dreary, monotone reality. Tada invites you to join his Revolution, but you must bring your own imagination. Tada can't be expected to take care of everything.

Susan has been crafting for as long as she can remember and was inspired by artists in her family. She has experimented with numerous art and craft techniques and disciplines, but mostly uses crochet and sewing, working with yarn and fabric.

Having trained and worked as an engineer until 2008, Susan is completely self-taught in her current practices, learning the basics from books, DVDs and the internet and going on to 'develop her own version and approach through experimentation and trial and error'. Susan finds inspiration in art, nature and everyday life. She comments:

Tada's Revolution follows the lives and adventures of stuffed animal characters in their 'natural' habitat. This parallel world is filled with wonder, mischief and conflict, and we observe how these characters interact, form relationships and handle universal experiences and challenges. It is our aim to produce genuine and authentic emotions and reactions, and to create these scenes with uncompromising meticulousness and attention to detail. The characters are meant to traverse the entire range of the human experience, from humour, excitement and empathy, to frustration, aggression and terror. It is my dream to recreate the world seen only in my imagination and share it with the world.

www.tadasrevolution.com

 LEFT TO RIGHT:
All pieces made by crochet, sewing and embroidery
using yarn, polyester fibrefill and glass eyes.

MR PEANUT GOES CAMPING
THE BAIT
BEARS OVER TROUBLED WATER
TEST DAY

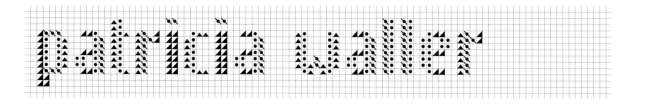

patricia waller

Patricia Waller was born in Santiago, Chile, but moved to Germany at a young age and went on to study fine art to Master's level. She has lectured in universities and art institutes in Germany and is based in Berlin.

Patricia got the idea for crocheting artwork during her final year of study of sculpture at the Academy of Fine Arts in Karlsruhe, Germany. She was looking for a material to work in that was not yet established in the art world and was also interested in working without the use of machines and electricity. She became a pioneer in Germany for the new craft-art movement, at a time when people, colleagues and contemporaries refused to take her approach seriously. She comments:

Wool is ranked low in art and art history. It is not the material of which major works of art were made, and it is considered feminine. If women artists deliberately work with it, we reflect our status in art, culture and society. Of course, I take advantage of the image of 'housewife art' so that, at first glance, my works appear innocent. On a closer look, however, people will discover a sort of vicious irony. If people start smiling or laughing at my work, I know that my first step of approaching them was successful.

Patricia has exhibited her work widely in Germany and Europe. Her work deals with serious themes of violence in society, fear, illness, disability and human fragility. It is also important to her to reflect serious topics in contemporary society such as family, religion, science, medicine and technology. Patricia says she strives to balance shock and banality in her work with projects such as 'How to Kill Your First Love' and juxtaposes the harmlessness and softness of wool with the severity and unexpectedness of her subject matter.

My ambiguous universe wrought from our turbulent modern existence is focused on art, commerce, technology and pop culture, and by now consists of numerous thematic blocks. In a subversive tongue-in-cheek manner, I mix together the absurd and the bizarre, careful observations of everyday life and an interest in humanity, to create these different phases of my work. In my works there is often a lot of blood. Blood, in this exaggerated and bizarre manner, stands in contrast to the material, wool. Due to the technique of crocheting and the selection of the subject matter, my works seem harmless at first sight. But if you take a closer look, you will discover biting irony and a strong dose of nastiness.

www.patriciawaller.com

▲ **CLOCKWISE FROM LEFT:**
MISS PIGGY
Yarn, wire, cotton wool, wood, synthetic material.

BICYCLE ACCIDENT
Yarn, synthetic material, metal.

UNICORN
Yarn, cotton wool, wire.

WHO KILLED BAMBI?
Yarn, fabric, cotton wool, synthetic material.

● **CLOCKWISE FROM LEFT:**
DUCK
Yarn, polystyrene, synthetic material.

SHARK
Yarn, wire.

FROM HEAVEN
Yarn, polystyrene, synthetic material, metal.

DOLL
Yarn, cotton wool, wood.

TWINS
Yarn, cotton wool.

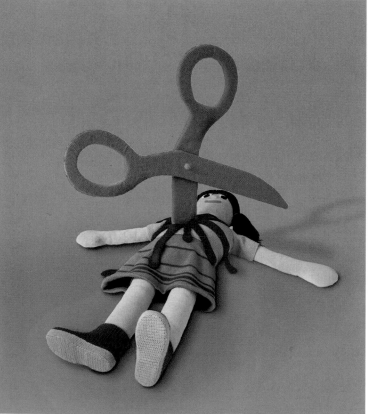

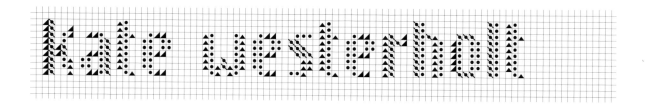

Kate Westerholt

Kate Westerholt is originally from Buffalo, New York, but has resided in London, England, for the past ten years. Her work is inspired by traditional cross stitch samplers. Samplers were used originally as a way of recording new stitches, patterns and motifs before pattern books existed. These designs were passed down through generations and are now regarded as pieces of decorative folk art in their own right. Kate is following the tradition and bringing it to a whole new audience after researching these traditional and recurring motifs and applying them in her own work.

Kate uses traditional materials – coloured cotton on cross stitch Aida fabric – and juxtaposes the traditional techniques and motifs with modern-day references such as film quotes, song lyrics and slang terms. She comments:

So many samplers that people have produced throughout history have used these same motifs or variations on them, but the text would denote values or interests from the time. For instance, Victorian samplers contained quotes from scriptures in the Bible. I wanted to do something that would, in a hundred years' time, give an insight into our society and popular culture today. I think that movies, song lyrics and street slang would be the memorable/memorized quotes of today, rather than Bible quotes or flowery verse. I don't know if that's generally a good thing, but I'm commenting on what's happening now. I also want to make people laugh; that is one of the most important aspects of my work. The humour comes from taking those traditional elements and combining them with a modern context.

One of Kate's pieces, 'Born Disco, Died Heavy Metal' shown over the page, uses the text from the lyrics of a Cornershop song. Kate adds:

The Adam and Eve motif is very old, possibly from as early as the 1600s. It's a typically religious image that I enjoyed juxtaposing with the modern text. For many people, music is their religion, and I see the words indicating a fall from innocence.

Kate has taken part in several prestigious group shows and has had work commissioned by British *Vogue*.

www.katewesterholt.com

CLOCKWISE FROM RIGHT:
All images cotton thread on 14 count Aida fabric.

GHETTO FABULOUS
WHEN I WAS YOUR AGE
BLESS THIS CRACK HOUSE

I WANNA ROCK AND ROLL ALL NIGHT

AND PARTY EVERY DAY

LEFT TO RIGHT:
Both cotton thread on 14 count Aida fabric.

ROCK AND ROLL
BORN DISCO, DIED HEAVY METAL

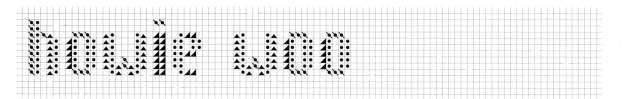

Howie Woo

Howie Woo is based in British Columbia, Canada, where he practises his 'Woo Work' – 3D Japanese amigurumi-style crocheted objects and animals. *Amigurumi* translates literally as 'knitted or crocheted stuffed doll'. Howie explains:

I crochet fun objects and photograph them to tell funny stories. My WooWork.com tagline is: Crochet creations for the playful at heart.

Howie has been crocheting since the summer of 2008, when his girlfriend began crocheting. His fascination with brightly coloured yarn, which began as a child, was reignited and he finally learned how to crochet through family and friends, books and the internet.

It isn't surprising when looking at Howie's photographs that he's dabbled with film school and art school (although found both environments too limiting and structured), and also practises illustration and photography. Howie's inspiration comes from his own childhood, inventing in crochet the kind of objects he dreamed of owning and playing with as an imaginative child, such as ray guns, UFOs and dynamite. His work process is unstructured and he doesn't use patterns – rather trial and error – to create each piece. He comments:

I choose what to crochet based on its qualities of fun and story: I like making fun objects that I've wanted to have since childhood, such as spy gadgets and sci-fi weaponry and a detachable nose. Lately, I've been enjoying the challenge of making imaginary objects that aren't found on Earth. I like to crochet objects that can, with the addition of photos, drawings and videos, tell an entertaining story, whether from my childhood or a current event or a make-believe adventure. I use all kinds of yarn: acrylic, wool and cotton. I usually choose my yarn based on colour. I sketch random objects and write story ideas in a notebook, then refine both before crocheting and photographing each project for my WooWork.com blog.

www.woowork.com

CLOCKWISE FROM LEFT:
All materials are crocheted in yarn
Photos of Howie: Mary Jane Kuhn.

NOSE DISGUISE
A.T.O.M.-A-THERAPY DEVICE RED ALERT
RAY GUN ALERT
RAY GUN FULL
RAY GUN CASE OPEN

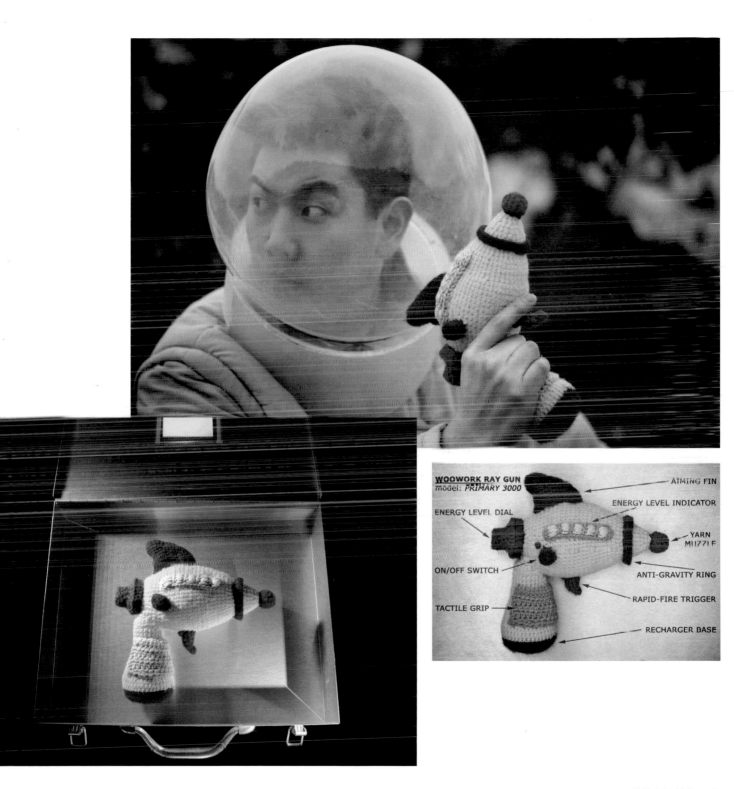

WOOWORK RAY GUN
model: *PRIMARY 3000*

ENERGY LEVEL DIAL

ON/OFF SWITCH

TACTILE GRIP

AIMING FIN

ENERGY LEVEL INDICATOR

YARN MUZZLE

ANTI-GRAVITY RING

RAPID-FIRE TRIGGER

RECHARGER BASE

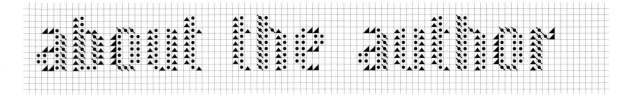

about the author

Jo Waterhouse is a freelance arts writer and author of the *Concrete to Canvas* books and *Art by Tattooists: Beyond Flash*. She lives in Worcester, England, with her artist husband, Chris Bourke, and is an avid Indie Crafter, dabbling with knitting, crochet, embroidery and whatever else she can get her hands on. She is the founding member of the Worcester Rebel Knitting Club and is one of the organizers of Worcester's Vintage & Craft Fair.

www.concretetocanvas.co.uk

Thanks and appreciation to:
Joaquima Casas Bo, Diem Chau, Susan Chi, Angela Chick, Debbie Daniel and East London Craft Guerrilla, Phil Davison, Erin Dollar, Marloes Dukyer, Jo Dunn, Jenny Hart, Kate Jenkins, Knit the City, Faythe Levine, Jacinta Lodge, Joetta Maue, Karen McClellan, Eva Monleón, Moxie, Sarah Neuburger, Tania Patritti, Emily Peacock, Shauna Richardson, Amy Rue, Naomi Ryder, Magda Sayeg, William Schaff, Severija, Matte Stephens, Vivienne Strauss, Patricia Waller, Kate Westerholt, Howie Woo, www.mrxstitch.com, and all at Laurence King Publishing.

All artwork remains the copyright of the artists.

● SELF-PORTRAIT by Jo Waterhouse
Hand embroidery and machine sewing and appliqué on cotton fabric scraps, embroidery floss.